For Karen

Contents

Appendix   **271**

Index   **285**

Preface

About the author

Malcolm Pryor is a member of the Society of Technical Analysts in the UK and has been designated a Certified Financial Technician by the International Federation of Technical Analysts.

He is a director of a consultancy practice, and is an expert at several games, including bridge where he has held the rank of Grandmaster for over a decade.

What this book covers

This is a book about financial spread betting. Although spread betting started way back in the 1970s, recent years have seen an explosion of interest, with increased demand for the product and new betting firms entering the marketplace. It is easy to open an account, and many people now have done so. Unfortunately, it is not so easy to make money.

What do successful spread bettors do that is different?

This book has been written to try to answer that question.

Who this book is for

This book is not for–

- complete beginners, it assumes a basic understanding of how spread betting works;

- people who think there is easy money out there, just waiting to be picked up;

- those who want to spread bet for the adrenalin rush, irrespective of the results.

Rather, the book has been written for people who want to have a serious go at spread betting, managing costs and risks, and who recognise that it will take some skill and effort.

If you are one of those people, this book will be of interest to you whether you have a spread betting account now, had one in the past, or are thinking of getting one in the future.

It is perfectly possible to spread bet just using the telephone. However, in this book I am assuming that all readers have a computer connected to the internet.

How this book is structured

Imagine a mountain called Spread Betting. Our mission is to climb it.

There are three key stages to climbing a mountain:

1. first a Base Camp must be established;

2. from there the journey up the mountain face begins; and

3. finally one makes an attempt on the summit.

This book reflects this three stage approach and is divided into three main parts. Let's expand on this a little.

We start with an Introduction which reviews some of the benefits of spread betting and highlights its current impressive growth.

Part I

In the first Part of the book, we set off to reach Base Camp. We review how to select a spread betting firm. We look at the hardware and software requirements to run a spread betting account and other resource requirements such as price data, information and web sites. We look at the timescales for making spread bets. We survey what winning spread bettors bet on and the types of instrument available. We review how the spread betting firms make their money, covering some controversial issues, including how prices are set, how competitive the market is, and whether the firms hedge our bets. We examine 10 common and really expensive errors spread bettors make. We highlight the importance of stop losses. We examine in detail the various different ways in which we can enter and exit bets and when to use each type of order. Finally we deal with some of the practical issues to do with running a spread bettng account.

We are now ready to climb the face of the mountain called Spread Betting.

Part II

In Part 2, we start to climb the Mountain. We outline various strategies that we could select for spread betting. We take a detailed look at the first strategy, betting on a trend, covering the basic concept, timeframes, identification of trends, weekly shortlists, daily set ups, entry triggers, position sizing, profit taking and re-entry. The next two strategies are then covered, betting on reversals, and in and out within a day; and we follow up by outlining a number of delta neutral strategies including pairs trading, arbitrage and hedging.

We are now ready to make our assault on the summit.

Part III

In Part 3, we set off on the route to the summit. We highlight the importance of the individual spread bettor in the equation, and we look at how the most successful spread bettors stay in control through planning, record keeping, regular reviews and various techniques of risk management. Part 3 concludes with a chapter on developing a winning attitude and a chapter on continual development.

Supporting web site

The publisher's web site supporting this book can be found at:
www.harriman-house.com/financialspreadbetting

The author's web site can be found at:
www.sparkdales.co.uk

Acknowledgements

I have many people to thank for providing support advice and encouragement to me while writing this book and I shall not be able to name them all personally; I really appreciate it, thanks.

I would like to thank the directors and staff of Harriman House for their help in publishing this book, especially Stephen Eckett who saw its potential and made it a much better book than it otherwise would have been.

I would like to thank the authors of the 25 books which have made the biggest impact on my own spread betting, whom I acknowledge in the final chapter.

I would like to thank Martin Stamp and Ionic Information Ltd for producing the ShareScope software and allowing it to be used to produce the charts in this book.

I would like to thank my fellow directors, shareholders and clients for their tolerance as I wrote this book, when I might have been doing other things.

And most of all I would like to thank Karen, to whom this book is dedicated.

Risk Warning

No responsibility for loss occasioned to any person or corporate body acting or refraining to act as a result of reading material in this book can be accepted by the Publisher or by the Author.

The information provided by the Author is not offered as, nor should it be inferred to be, advice or recommendation to readers, since the financial circumstances of readers will vary greatly and investment or trading behaviour which may be appropriate for one reader is unlikely to be appropriate for others.

Introduction

What's special about spread betting?

It probably won't come as a surprise that I am a fan of spread betting. Its attractions include–

Spread betting is very straight-forward

The mechanics of entering or exiting bets are straightforward. Since this is supposed to be a relatively advanced book on spread betting, for the most part I will assume everyone is familiar with the basics of how spread betting works. The firms' web sites and marketing literature provide easy to follow explanations of the mechanics. (In case you feel you need a refresher, some basic bets are illustrated and basic terms explained in the Appendix).

Open to everyone

You can open a spread betting account with just a few hundred pounds.

Credit available

Spread betting firms often allow credit facilities – although these may be unsuitable for some people.

Exposure to a wide range of markets

You can bet on commodities, interest rates, bonds, stocks, indices and currencies – all of which can be traded from the one account. And if that's not enough there is also betting on sports and politics – it seems like you can bet on almost anything today.

Ability to go short

You can bet on stocks falling in price. Before spread betting came along, shorting stocks wasn't easy for ordinary investors. With spread betting, shorting is as easy as going long. Shorting is not a natural activity for many new traders, but trading without shorting is like trading with one hand tied behind your back.

No Tax

You make money and you don't pay tax on it – that can't be bad! However, there is a double edged sword here in that if you have trading losses you can't offset your losses against any capital gains you might have elsewhere. Also, the tax advantages are not much use if you don't make any profits, or if your profits are less than the capital gains threshold.

Low transaction costs

No stamp duty and no commissions! These costs can really mount up if you actively trade the underlying instruments direct. However, you will generally find the spreads in spread betting are higher, offsetting some of the advantages regarding stamp duty and commissions.

Remove currency exposure

With some firms you can bet on, say, a US stock in pounds per point rather than dollars per point. So you don't have to worry about the dollar going up or down in addition to worrying about the price movement of the instrument.

Sophisticated trading platforms

Most spread betting firms have invested heavily in their trading platforms, which offer sophisticated risk and account management tools, charting, analysis and news as part of the service.

Leverage

Spread betting can offer extreme leverage. For instance, you can bet on an index, or on one of the larger FTSE 100 stocks, with only 3% margin.

Let's take BHP Billiton as an example, with the stock trading at 1100p. You can have exposure to the equivalent of £1100 worth of BHP Billiton stock with just £33 of money in your account. Or £11,000 worth of stock with £330. Or £110,000 worth with £3,300. But with such leverage comes high risk, which is one of the topics we look at later.

Overlap and convergence of betting products

Recent developments in sports betting are now starting to spill over into the financial spread betting world. In sports betting there are three ways to bet:

1. **fixed odds betting** (e.g. the traditional bet at the bookie's),

2. **betting exchanges** (where in general the odds are more favourable than using a bookie, and where you can get to play the bookie by laying as well as backing results), and

3. sports **spread betting**.

In the financial arena, betting exchanges haven't as yet taken off, but could do one day; fixed odds betting, particularly in the form of binary betting, is growing.

This book is mainly about financial spread betting. We do take a quick look at exchange betting and binary betting, but don't spend a huge amount of time on them; in the case of exchange betting because it hasn't got going yet in the financial arena, and in the case of binary betting because the product range is currently fairly limited (major indices are well covered for instance but not FTSE250 stocks), the upside is too limited, and it is too difficult to get a consistent winning edge. We do look briefly at some innovative fixed odds betting products which have potential. But our main focus is on financial spread betting.

One million spread bettors

Spread betting is growing rapidly. One recent estimate put the number of customers at between a quarter and half a million, with expected growth to in excess of one million over the next 5 years.

Climbing the spread betting mountain

You can peer at the Summit of the Spread Betting Mountain in the distance and dream of riches, but if you spread bet without knowing what you are doing you will be like a climber setting off to climb a mountain with no preparation, no protective clothing, no equipment and no guide. This book won't guarantee you success but I do hope that it will plug some of those gaps.

PART 1

Base Camp

Part 1 – Base Camp

If we want to climb the mountain called Spread Betting, our first task is to reach Base Camp. Getting to Base Camp means we will have the requisite background knowledge and resources to start spread betting. More specifically, we will know how to select a spread betting firm; we will have identified the resources we need by way of hardware, software, price data, information and web sites. We will have formed a view on what underlying instruments we wish to bet on, and have an understanding of the various spread betting products on the market. We will have respect for the dangers of spread betting and understand where many spread bettors go wrong. We will have enhanced our safety by appreciating the merits of stop losses; and we will have a good understanding of the various methods of entering and exiting bets. When we get to Base Camp we will already be better equipped than many spread bettors.

1

Choosing A
Spread Betting Firm

Before we start to spread bet we need a spread betting account. This chapter provides a little background to the spread betting market and then looks at how to select a spread betting firm. If you are an experienced spread bettor with more than one account you may find you know most of this material and can whizz through it.

Origins and growth of the market

IG Index – the first spread betting firm

The first spread betting firm was IG Index, who set up a facility in 1974 for people to bet on the price of gold (when there were restrictions on buying gold outright). They also introduced betting on a number of other financial instruments.

Over time, other firms entered the market and the range of the futures-style products on offer expanded. Sports betting was also introduced. The spread betting market expanded rapidly from the end of the 1990s as both demand (new customers) and supply (new spread betting firms) increased.

Deal4free introduce rolling daily bets

The market changed somewhat when the firm currently trading as CMC Markets entered it (trading at that time as Deal4free). Firstly, because they had an open and aggressive strategy of undercutting the other firms' spreads and, secondly, because they marketed a new product, the rolling daily bet. Rolling daily bets are settled each day, but the positions are automatically carried over to the next day ("rolled over") until closed with interest being charged or credited on a daily basis as long as the bet remains open. As well as the tight spreads, customers using these new products got increased transparency, given that the Deal4free price was clearly based on the cash price in the market, rather than a price adjusted for future interest and dividends.

In the last few years there have been a number of further new entrants to the market so that at the last count there were a couple of dozen firms offering spread betting services.

This increase, combined with increasing customer sophistication, has resulted in a much more competitive market, which has had a number of beneficial consequences for the customers. Spreads have tightened, and are continuing to tighten, as customers are increasingly willing and able to switch accounts.

Trading platforms have improved significantly and service quality, seen as critical, has improved.

On a personal note, I have preferred over the years to have accounts with more than one firm. In fact, with many of them. It is helpful to:

- see who is currently offering the tightest spreads,

- keep up with new product offerings, and

- make sure I can always place the bets I want in the volume I want.

I have occasionally found that one firm won't take any new bets on a particular instrument, for whatever reason, while another firm is still open for business in that instrument.

Selection criteria

Choosing a spread betting provider will depend to some extent on your personal preferences. In particular, these preferences will impact on the weightings you put on the main criteria:

1. range of products,

2. are the specific products you want available?

3. tightness of spreads,

4. general functionality, such as quality of order automation (e.g. stops),

5. trading software/web site – quality of extras (e.g. news, fundamentals, technicals),

6. quality of phone trading service,

7. quality of trade execution, back office and customer service, and

8. additional benefits (e.g. interest paid on funds in the account).

For my own betting, two of these criteria stand out as being significantly more important than the others-

1. Specific product (rolling daily bet)

I want a specific product to be available (the rolling daily bet product), since that is my favourite type of instrument. This is my preference. Maybe in your case it is the binary bet product that is most important, or the less common commodity futures products, or something else.

2. Size of spread

The tightness of spreads is critical to me, since that has a big impact on my style of trading over the course of a year. The trading software is of course also important, however I could personally live with an inferior platform that had tight spreads in preference to an all singing all dancing platform with inferior spreads.

The back office and customer service support has in my experience been helpful and reliable from all the firms I have dealt with.

> At various times customers have received PDAs, free bets, and champagne. By all means enjoy them if you get them, but base your selection on all the criteria, not just the giveaways.

Once in a while one of the firms embarks on a marketing campaign giving away freebies.

The 6-Stage Plan for opening an account

There are six key stages to work through when opening a spread betting account-

1. Inspect the **marketing literature** and advertisements; the larger firms advertise regularly in the weekly investment magazines.

2. Look at the **web sites** to see which ones you like best and check **product ranges.**

3. Check out the size of the **spreads.**

4. Talk to **current users** to get their feedback. You can also get some idea by looking at comments on internet bulletin boards – although do be careful here, one disgruntled client can make a lot of noise, whereas satisfied clients tend to keep quiet.

5. **Visit the spread betting firm** – most will show you around their shop, and you can pick up the vibes.

6. Open **more than one account,** for flexibility.

There are a few additional points that may be important for some traders and not others, such as-

- minimum account size – varies from £100 to £5000;

- availability of **credit facilities**;

- **margin structure** – varies from 1% with one firm for some indices up to 20% or more for smaller stocks with another;

- quality of **training material**; and

- ability to **practice on a dummy account or with very small bet sizes** in a real account – at the time of writing one firm (Finspreads) allows bets of 1p per point for an initial period.

Directory of spread betting firms

A directory of spread betting firms can be found in the appendix to this book.

We now know how to select a spread betting firm. The next chapter looks at more setting up issues: computer requirements.

2

Getting Set Up – Computer Hardware And Software

This chapter looks at the spread bettor's computer requirements. If you have recently purchased a computer and consider yourself well versed in operating it you may want to speed read this section.

Back in the early part of the last century some of the greatest traders that have ever lived, such as Jesse Livermore, made fortunes betting on the movement of stocks and commodities. The technology they had to help them was primitive to say the least: paper charts, the ticker tape of the most recent trades, telegrams, phones, prices written up on a board on the wall as they came through on the tape. It is possible that people today make money out of spread betting without a computer, but I am prepared to bet their numbers will be small. If you can get an edge just looking at paper charts, that's great. But for most of us the computer is an essential tool for spread betting.

Hardware

The good news is that computers get more powerful every year, and also cheaper.

You have an existing computer

If you have an old or low spec PC you should check with any potential spread betting firm you are applying to what the minimum computer specification they need for you to use their software.

Having phoned around all my current spread betting accounts, it would appear that 0.8 GHz processor, 256 KB RAM, plus 100 MB free disk space is about the most any of them say they need you to have.

Several of the firms add that they require the PC to be Java enabled, and several others require Flashplayer (from Macromedia). But if you get a CD off them this is likely to get sorted during the software download, and even if it doesn't it's no great problem to fix.

An old PC I recently abandoned (which, needless to say, appeared very high powered when I bought it in 2000!), had a very low spec by today's standards but has been fine for all my spread betting, real time data and end of day data downloads.

So, if you already have a computer that's connected to the internet and you're happy with it, then in all likelihood it will be fine for online spread betting. On the other hand, if you're thinking of buying a new computer anyway, some notes follow.

Recommendation

If you have an old computer that seems slow, sometimes just adding more memory (RAM) can significantly speed the computer up.

You're thinking of buying a new computer

Computer technology is racing ahead, but it is being driven by the requirements of multimedia as computers morph into entertainment centres. By contrast, the computing requirements for trading are very modest. And the real cost of computers today is very low, such that if any person finds their cost significant or worrying then there's a strong argument that they shouldn't be spread betting.

> To cut to the chase, it is virtually impossible to buy a computer today – even at the lowest prices – that is not powerful enough for spread betting and active trading generally.

Having recently upgraded from an ancient PC to a more modern laptop, I had to update my knowledge a little bit. The spec I went for: a laptop with 2.6 GHz Speed, 1600 MHz BUS, 1000 KB Cache, 1024 MB memory, 100 GB storage plus most of the extras and a bit of software thrown in. This is way more than I actually need for spread betting. But in a couple of years anyone reading this will no doubt be amused at such a low spec.

Recommendation

The two key recommendations I would make are-

1. Don't skimp on the on the computer's memory (RAM). Get at least 1GB of RAM and 2GB if you can afford it.

2. Don't necessarily buy the cheapest computer, or the one with the best deal. There are other factors, besides price, that are more important. For example, if you are not confident with your computer skills, then it is a good idea to buy a computer that offers good after sales support.

References

Some web sites with information on buying computers:

compreviews.about.com/cs/desktops/bb/aabybdesktops.htm

www.infohq.com/Computer/computer-buying-primer.htm

www.css.msu.edu/PC-Guide/PC-Guide1.cfm

Internet connection

Today, having a computer with no internet connection is like owning a car in a country with no road network.

Ideally, you should have a broadband internet connection. Not that spread betting requires it, it's just much more convenient. Where I live, no one has broadband, so I have to make do with a miserable 56K max phone line. If you are in this boat, fear not, most things seem to work OK. But obviously if a spread betting firm gives you a choice of an internet download to get their trading platform (likely to take well over an hour at that speed) or a CD in the post, take the CD!

References

- Broadband Checker (www.broadbandchecker.co.uk) – good quick explanation of broadband
- ADSL Guide (www.adslguide.org.uk) – test your connection speed

General software

Some general software recommendations

- **MS Office** (including Word and Excel). Excel is particularly useful for portfolio monitoring. If you don't want to pay the high price for MS Office (approx £300), then MS Works is OK, but much better is OpenOffice (www.openoffice.org) which has 99% of the functionality of MS Office but is free.

- **AVG Anti-Virus** (www.grisoft.com). Norton and McAfee are the leading anti-virus programs, but AVG is just as good, with less annoyances and is free.

- **Spybot** (www.spybot.info). Keep track of spyware on your computer.

- **CCleaner** (www.ccleaner.com). Great, free utility that deletes all those files that gunge up Windows computers (i.e. temp files, cookies, deleted files etc.)

Backing up

Amazingly, I still come across people who have lost all their data because their computer died. This really shouldn't happen, as today backing up is very cheap and simple. A couple of methods to consider-

1. Back up regularly onto CD or DVD if you have a CD burner.

2. Buy an external hard disk and back up onto that. These hard disks plug into a USB port and work just like an ordinary hard drive. Go to www.amazon.co.uk, and drill down to "Electronics & Photo › Computer Peripherals › Drives & Storage" for a quick overview of the range and prices for hard drives.

Postscript

We now have a spread betting account and a computer. But there are other resources we need before we can start, which we look at in the next chapter.

3

Trading Resources

This chapter looks at further resources we may need to spread bet: trading software, price data, information and web sites.

Trading software

Cost issues

I have made an assumption on hardware that in today's world pretty nearly everyone who is going to spread bet is going to have a PC, so in a sense the PC isn't an incremental cost for the spread bettor.

When it comes to trading software on the other hand, costs start to be a factor. You should consider software costs to be part of your overall spread betting profit and loss account. So if you only have £500 in your spread betting account you are going to find it much harder to make a profit if you spend £450 a year on software and related data downloads. And yet good software can help you win.

Vicious circle or what?

Apart from costs, the other key factor to consider with software is what we want to do with it.

Functionality

First up, we want to make spread bets and to monitor them. The good news here is the spread betting firms' software comes as part of the service, and in addition to providing the means to make the actual bets online, and to manage them, most of the firms provide a wealth of extras on their sites. You should take a tour of the sites to get a feel for what is on offer for each firm's customers. This tends to include: news, access to some fundamental data, technical analysis and market prices. If you have a small account and want to keep all costs to a minimum, you could get by with just using your spread betting firms' sites, supplemented with access to one or two of the free financial web sites outlined later in this chapter.

But we can do better by spending money on trading software.

Trading software programs

Here is a list of some the major trading software programs around-

- Equis (www.equis.com)

- eSignal (www.esignal.com)

- ShareScope (www.sharescope.co.uk)

- SimplyChart (www.simplychart.com)

- Updata (www.updata.com)

Personally, I use ShareScope, which I describe in some detail below.

ShareScope

Most people find that they need access to specialist software facilitating detailed analysis of end of day historical data. The charts in this book were produced using a program called ShareScope. Under prices applicable when writing this chapter, the cost of the end of day service is £14 per month after a one off £79.95 joining fee. For this you get the software (and free upgrades), historic data going back a decade or more in some cases, plus a download each trading day of the latest prices.

I have been using the ShareScope software since 2001 and have found that the additional analytical capability that it gives me is well worth the annual costs. Specifically, what I get from it over and above what I can get from the free sites includes the following:

1. easier to navigate round all the instruments, (e.g. can flick through all constituents of the FTSE 350 one at a time with one keystroke per stock);

2. more flexibility in sorting instruments (e.g. by volatility, today's price change, market cap);

3. easier to switch timeframes (e.g. from daily to weekly to monthly at a key stroke);

4. easier to customise chart styles (e.g. candles, point and figure, bar charts);

5. more comprehensive set of indicators (over 60);

6. easier to vary parameters of indicators;

7. easier to personalise specific charts (e.g. draw support and resistance, trend lines, add notes etc)

8. more flexibility in creating portfolios of instruments;

9. much faster response, since once you have downloaded the data the software is off-line; and

10. more flexible filtering system (i.e Data Mining).

Having looked at software, next on our shopping list of resources for spread betting is price data.

Price data

With ShareScope, effectively you buy the software first then you pay a regular fee for receiving price data. This is typically how all the trading software providers operate. So far, we have looked at end of day data. But there is also more expensive data available for those that need it – intraday price data.

This comes in two main types:

1. delayed – data is usually delayed by 20 minutes.

2. real time – data is streamed to you computer in real-time with no delay,

Delayed vs. real time intraday data

With either you are able to look at intraday patterns and trends on a much smaller time frame than a day; commonly used timeframes are hourly, half hourly, 15 minute, 10 minute and 5 minute. On a 15 minute chart for instance each bar represents 15 minutes of trading.

How expensive is intraday data?

A number of the spread betting firms supply real time data for free for account holders (although sometimes the data is based on their prices rather than the underlying market); you can get delayed intraday data for free from a number of web sites; you can also get intraday day via the trading software programs mentioned earlier in this chapter.

Let's have a quick look at the costs of buying this data from a software supplier, using ShareScope as an example:

1. delayed intraday data costs £28 per month (compared with £14 per month for end of day),

2. real time data costs £84.95 per month.

So, why get intraday data?

Three main reasons.

1. If you are betting in day trading mode, betting on small intraday movements, you must be able to spot trends and patterns that occur during the day. In this case you almost certainly need real time data, since a 20 minute delay may mean you are late spotting key developments. You had better have a big account and be very skilful, otherwise the costs of this data will be impossible to overcome.

2. You may find that understanding the intraday trends and patterns helps you fine tune your entries and exits on the longer time frames e.g. daily.

3. If you have real time data, with live bid and ask prices, you can keep a reality check on the prices from your spread betting firm.

With these last two reasons, you have to be clear that the potential benefits are worth the costs.

My personal solution

Mainly for the second and the third reasons (listed above), my personal solution to this issue is as follows:

1. Delayed intraday data

For an extra £14 per month I have delayed intraday data from ShareScope which allows me to look at 10 days of 30 minute charts, 15 minute charts and 5 minute charts, and thereby fine tune my entries and exits. I calculate that the improvements in timing I obtain comfortably cover the costs; plus I get some additional functionality in the software thrown in.

2. Real time data

I have an account with myBroker.com, an online broker, which provides real time data and a range of other facilities for a little over £400 per year. With this I can see the current "yellow strip" (the range of best bid and best offer in the market place) and I won't place bets on a market order with any spread betting firm if they are significantly out of line with this. I will either place a limit order to get the price I want (or pass on the bet), or I will use another firm who are more in line with the yellow strip.

Penny pinching?

Yes indeed, and over the year it comes to a lot of pennies, certainly a lot more than the costs of the real time data. I also find the myBroker.com real time portfolio monitoring functionality excellent. I key in to it my trade plan each day, with notes of potential entries, stops and targets, and can set audio and email alarms for when any of these get triggered.

Your solution

You have to do the sums for your own situation.

A small account can't absorb significant data costs – no problem, you can win without them.

For bigger accounts, you need to work out whether the potential gains for your style of trading outweighs the costs. For many people they won't, so don't waste money on delayed or real time data if it's not going to improve your overall profit.

Level 2

For a further outlay you can obtain Level 2 data.

Here are some of the more useful pieces of information which come with Level 2 on the London Stock Exchange:

1. **Last traded price** (plus trade type and time and volume for the trade).

2. Price and type of the **last 5 trades** (plus volume and value of each trade).

3. **Highest and lowest prices** of the day.

4. **VWAP** – volume weighted average price of today's trading (this is particularly useful since it helps understand where within the day's range the bulk of trading has taken place).

5. **Buy and sell volume** (how many shares are being offered on the order book).

6. **Yellow strip** (the best buy and sell prices, the number of orders at those prices and the volume of shares available).

7. Analysis of the **order book** (two columns showing buy and sell orders and quotes at each price, showing volume of shares available) – you can either see all the orders, or (my preference) see a summary where only one line per price is displayed. The advantage of this is that you can see how many

unfilled orders there are above and below the current price, whether there are any imbalances which might in the very short term push the price up or down.

For ShareScope customers who already pay for intraday data (delayed or real time) it costs an extra £25 per month.

Once again, the key thing is to compare benefits and costs – will the benefits of Level 2 data outweigh the incremental costs? For many spread bettors (including myself) the answer will be no. However, there are a growing number of traders who find they can harness the power of this information to improve the timing of their entries and exits enough to justify the costs.

What to do if you are away from your PC

There is one more topic to cover on price data.

You have worked out what data you want downloaded to your PC. But what about when you are not at your PC? What if you want to know what is going on when you are nowhere near your PC? There are several solutions to this problem:

1. Going away for a long time? I personally prefer to exit all bets, so I don't need the data. It's good to take a break, I am unlikely to be able to manage my bets properly while I am away, and if they go against me it spoils the holiday; at the very least if I keep any bets open I will ensure that every bet has an automated stop loss on it.

2. For shorter periods, again automated stops allow you to exit even though you are unable to monitor the bets personally.

3. Most firms are happy for you to phone in occasionally to check prices; make it clear you are not intending to trade and don't call in too often.

4. If you can get internet access then you can check prices on the internet (don't forget to take your login/password with you!).

5. Data downloads to phone or PDA are possible and with some firms you can also trade from them.

6. You can phone in to some data providers – and to at least one spread betting firm – and get prices without having to talk to anyone. Speech recognition technology is used in some cases.

Information

As we found for software, so it is for information – there's some free stuff out there, and there's stuff you pay for. Again, as for software, treat any information you pay for as part of your spread betting profit and loss, make sure the benefits outweigh the costs, and if your account size is small you will have to be economical. Here is a view of how I personally navigate my way through this.

Free stuff, web sites

The source of the free stuff is, as before, the spread betting firms' sites and the free parts of the various financial web sites out there, some of which I list in the next section.

Magazines

As general background material I subscribe to three weekly magazines (*Investors Chronicle*, *Shares* and *Money Week*) and one monthly one (*Traders'*). This costs me about £350 per year, and I suspect I could make do with just

> I never ever trade off any tips any of these magazines provide. For me it's strictly background material, helping me stay in tune with the markets.

Traders' plus one of the weekly magazines. The Investors Chronicle and Shares subscriptions also cover access to parts of a couple of useful web sites. I personally don't bother with a daily paper.

Newsletters

There are hundreds of advisory letters and subscription based web sites out there, and it's not my style to pay money for that kind of thing. I prefer to pack my own parachute, in a manner of speaking.

OK, there is one exception here that proves the rule. I subscribe to John Murphy's newsletter from the stockcharts.com web site, which comes out several times a week and covers key inter market trends primarily from a U.S. perspective. It costs me about £100 per year at current exchange rates. A number of John Murphy's books are featured in Part 3, in my list of the twenty five books I have learnt the most from. I also receive a number of free daily and weekly emails.

Web sites

There are a large number of web sites devoted to financial information, trading, news and so on. Some are subscription based, others are free (although with some of them you do have to go through the process of signing up as a member first.) For my style of trading I don't spend a huge amount of time trawling through web sites, and my needs for price data are filled through my subscription based software. So the list of web sites I use for spread betting is very small.

Web sites I use regularly

- www.moneyam.com – I have access to this by virtue of being a Shares magazine subscriber and I mainly use this site to look at reports on breaking news, for example company results just out or interest rate decisions.

- www.stockcharts.com – I subscribe to the John Murphy newsletter which is accessed via this site, I also find the free parts of this site helpful, particularly the charts on overall worldwide market trends.

Web sites providing free charts and prices

- www.advfn.com
- www.bigcharts.com
- www.ft.com
- www.marketwatch.com
- uk.finance.yahoo.com

Sites I use of more general educational interest:

www.iitm.com – The site of Dr Van Tharp and contains references to his various books and training material; you can sign up for a periodic newsletter of great interest to traders.

www.sta-uk.org – The site of the Society of Technical Analysts.

Postscript

This has been quite a detailed chapter. Now we have a spread betting account and a computer and we have selected a range of other resources. We know that whatever we spend on these other resources forms part of our overall spread betting profit and loss account; and therefore before we spend our precious funds on software, data, subscription web sites, magazines or newsletters we must think carefully whether we will gain from them more than they cost.

But what are we going to bet on?

That's what we look at in the next chapter.

4

What Do Winning Spread Bettors Bet On?

This chapter runs through the many types of instruments available to bet on and discusses some of the things winners are looking for when they decide what to bet on.

Although individual stocks and stock indices are popular with the spread betting community, there is a very wide range of potential instruments to bet on.

Some spread bettors restrict themselves to just trading one type of instrument, for example FTSE100 shares. But if your trading system depends on, say, trending markets, it's sensible to look at a wide range of instruments. If stocks are trending you can bet on stocks. If stocks seem range-bound, but several currencies are trending well, you can bet on those currencies. Currencies unclear? Maybe oil or gold or some other commodity is moving.

Markets

The available instruments generally fall into the following categories-

1. commodities

2. currencies

3. indices

4. stocks

5. other

I describe these in some detail below.

ETFs

bonds

Binary

Option

House Price

1. Commodities

Historically, oil and gold have been popular bets. Customer interest in commodities is on the increase and most firms will be positioning themselves to offer commodity related bets if they haven't done so already. The main categories of commodity that you can bet on are-

• precious metals (e.g. gold, silver, platinum),

• industrial metals (e.g. copper, zinc),

• oil related (e.g. Brent crude),

• agricultural (e.g. wheat, corn),

- livestock (e.g. pork bellies, cattle), and

- tropicals (e.g. soya beans, coffee).

Some firms allow bets on commodity related indices, such as the Reuters Jefferies Commodity CRB price index.

When betting on commodities it is essential to know:

1. What type of underlying contract the spread betting firm is basing their price on (e.g. futures based or spot, UK based or US based, £ or in $).

2. What unit the spread betting firm is using for bet size (e.g. £ per ounce). This will usually be based on the underlying contract, but you should always check.

2. Currencies

Interest in currencies has grown over the last few years, and most firms have either introduced or will be introducing currency bets. The more obvious currency pairs are the most popular, and spot is more popular than forward-

- USD/JPY – dollar yen

- EUR/USD – euro dollar

- GBP/USD – sterling dollar (sometimes called 'cable')

- EUR/GBP – euro sterling.

But there is a much wider selection than that. Check out the web sites.

I hesitate to mention this in a non-beginners' book, but **traders do occasionally get their currencies back to front, for instance selling GBP/USD when they expect the dollar to decline. Write out the bet first to avoid basic errors like this.**

As with commodities, make sure you know what unit the firm is using for bet size. For instance, cable is usually in pounds per pip (or basis point), which means if you expect the dollar to decline and buy GBP/USD at 1.6222 at £1 per point your account will move up or down £1 every time GBP/USD moves by 0.0001. Your bet size is equivalent to buying £16,222 of the underlying financial instrument.

3. Indices

All the firms do these, and all the old favourites are available on a futures or a cash market basis, (e.g. FTSE 100, Dow Jones Industrials, Nikkei, CAC40, DAX). Again, usually there is a much wider selection available, which you can see on the web sites.

A number of the firms use colloquial terms for some of the indices, for instance calling the Dow Jones Industrials "New York" or the DAX "Germany".

4. Stocks

Most firms do all the FTSE 100 constituents. Some do the FTSE 350 constituents as well. Not all do smaller stocks, and of those some have a minimum company size limit based on capitalisation (e.g. £50 million). The bigger firms do the larger overseas stocks.

What is available to bet on is, generally speaking, expanding – for the latest information always check with the spread betting firm. If there is something you want to bet on but can't find it listed on the web site, some firms will be prepared to give you a quote on the phone nonetheless.

5. Other

Several firms allow you to bet on options (call or put). This should strictly be for the experienced, and watch out with UK options. The spreads in the underlying market are scary and inevitably they filter through to the spread bets. (I am looking forward one day to meeting someone who makes a regular profit out of spread betting on options. Maybe they are out there somewhere, but I've never met them.)

You can bet on **bonds** and on **interest rate** futures with a number of firms.

You can bet on the VIX (the Chicago Board Options Exchange Volatility Index) with a number of firms. The VIX is calculated from a weighted basket of options on the S&P 500 index, and is widely used as a barometer of market sentiment.

Some firms have in the past provided their customers opportunities to invest in upcoming **initial public offerings** by offering a grey market in shares of a new market listing.

Several firms offer bets on **sectors** within the UK stock market.

Several of the spread betting firms have moved into the **fixed odds** betting arena, or its equivalent the **binary bet**.

There are a wide range of non financial bets available including sports bets and high profile one offs – such as the number of seats won by a particular party in an election, or the number of weeks a prime minister has remaining in No 10. You could at one stage bet on housing indices with IG Index.

In general, the spread betting firms are on the look out for new areas of customer interest, and if there is something that the customers are going to want to bet on they are likely to want to offer it.

The 3 key tests

There are three things to look for when picking which of the many instruments to bet on: volatility, liquidity and the spread.

1. Volatility

Some instruments have a tendency to move much more than others, and, very simplistically, that is really what we mean by volatility in this context. It might sound an obvious thing to say, but when you make a bet on something you want it to move after you have made the bet.

Mean reversion

Volatility tends to be mean reverting. In other words, the level of volatility in an instrument fluctuates – after a lot of movement the instrument is likely to have a more stable period and vice versa, and so the prevailing volatility tends to return to the historic average. You can see this visually if you put a study called Bollinger bands on your charts; the width of the bands expands and contracts as the volatility of the instrument increases or decreases over your selected time frame.

Volatility of different markets

Volatility varies by instrument too. There are various measures for calculating this volatility, for instance with ShareScope end of day data you can get a comparative measure for all instruments using the standard deviation of the natural logarithm of (current close / previous close) multiplied by 100. The result is a number that can be compared to any other instrument that has volatility calculated in the same way. Below is a table of volatility levels for a random selection of instruments to give an idea of how volatility differs between the them. A higher figure means greater volatility.

Table 4.1: volatility levels for a selection of markets

Note: The popular perception is that currencies have a high volatility, but this

Name	Code	Volatility
Regus Group PLC	RGU	6.17
Autonomy Corporation PLC	AU.	4.75
ARM Holdings PLC	ARM	4.58
PartyGaming PLC	PRTY	4.25
Corus Group PLC	CS.	3.82
Cookson Group PLC	CKSN	3.22
Sage Group (The) PLC	SGE	2.75
British Airways PLC	BAY	2.46
BHP Billiton PLC	BLT	2.44
Vodafone Group PLC	VOD	2.39
FTSE Fixed Line Telecommunications	NMX6530	2.21
HBOS PLC	HBOS	2.09
Barclays PLC	BARC	1.99
Silver (LBM) $	S$	1.78
Tesco PLC	TSCO	1.68
Hang Seng	HSI	1.64
BP PLC	BP.	1.63
DAX (Xetra)	DAX	1.56
Nikkei 225	NIK	1.42
Land Securities Group PLC	LAND	1.27
S&P 500	GSPC	1.12
Dow Jones Industrial Average	DJI	1.09
FTSE 350 Construction & Materials	NMX2350	1.09
FTSE 100	UKX	1.07
Gold (LBM) $	G$	1.05
USD/AUD - Australian $ per US$	USDAUD	0.69
GBP/USD - US $ per £	GBPUSD	0.53
GBP/EUR - Euros per £	GBPEUR	0.45

Source: ShareScope data

is not the case, as can be seen in the table. What *does* have a high volatility are currency trades which are often very highly leveraged (i.e. it is the trade and not the underlying instrument that is volatile).

Using the ShareScope methodology, if an instrument has a volatility reading of 1.5 this implies (assuming the future is in line with the past) that there is a 95% chance that a daily change in the price of the instrument will be less than 3% of the price. However, it is not important to understand the details of these calculations; the benefit of these volatility figures is that they give us a straightforward comparative ranking of the volatility of each instrument.

In general, I prefer the higher volatility instruments for spread betting because they are on average likely to move further quicker. So, with reference to the above table, I would prefer betting on say Corus Group PLC than on Land Securities. We will revisit this table after we have looked at the other two key tests.

2. Liquidity

It is safer betting on instruments where the underlying instrument (the share, commodity, currency, or other asset that you are betting on) has good liquidity – in other words, it is heavily traded.

The danger of betting on an asset with little liquidity is that you can get caught out if you need to exit in a hurry. Suppose you are long of a small cap stock and it moves against you. You want to exit. But if everyone else trading that stock that day has the same idea as you – they want to exit – you can find the stock has a violent move down.

Generally there is plenty of liquidity in indices, FTSE 100 stocks, the larger FTSE 250 stocks (especially if traded via SETS), the major currency pairs (e.g. dollar yen, dollar sterling, sterling euro) and the major commodities (e.g. gold and oil). I prefer to stick with the more liquid instruments because I want to be able to exit my bet slickly and relatively painlessly when I have to.

3. Spread

The bigger the spread (difference between bid and offer prices) the more success we need with our bet just to reach breakeven. If we are aiming to catch quite small moves of say 5%, or even less, it is going to make our life a lot harder if we lose 2% on the spread.

This is another reason why I stick with the bigger, more liquid instruments – they tend to have tighter spreads. **I reject many potential bets because I am just not interested if the spread is more than 1% on a round trip basis** (i.e. ½% on the entry and ½% on the exit).

On a rolling daily bet on a FTSE 100 stock you should be getting close to the yellow strip – which should be a lot less than a 1% spread.

As an example, I have just been quoted 1996p-1999p for Reckitt Benkiser – a 3 point spread, and 2137p-2139p for Anglo American, a 2 point spread. These are spreads of 0.15% and just under 0.1% respectively. These sorts of spreads help keep the costs of your betting down. At this game, it pays to watch the costs.

Putting it all together

Here is our volatility table again, but re-sorted with some extra columns: a snapshot of spreads for each instrument; the spread expressed as a percentage of the price; and the volatility expressed as a multiple of the spread percentage. We want to bet on volatile instruments with low spreads, so we are looking for a high ratio in this last column.

Table 4.2: comparison of spreads to volatility

Name	Code	Volatility	Spread	Spread as a % of price	Volatility to spread multiple
Cookson Group PLC	CKSN	3.22	549.25/50.00	0.05	64
DAX (Xetra)	DAX	1.56	5864/66	0.03	52
HBOS PLC	HBOS	2.09	1009.00/.50	0.05	42
British Airways PLC	BAY	2.46	422.00/.25	0.06	41
Hang Seng	HSI	1.64	17227/34	0.04	41
FTSE 100	UKX	1.07	5958/60	0.03	36
Corus Group PLC	CS.	3.82	399.25/.75	0.13	29
S&P 500	GSPC	1.12	1310.2/10.7	0.04	28
Dow Jones Industrial Average	DJI	1.09	11449/54	0.04	27
GBP/USD - US $ per £	GBPUSD	0.53	1.8872/75	0.02	27
Barclays PLC	BARC	1.99	664.00/.50	0.08	25
BHP Billiton PLC	BLT	2.44	1027/8	0.10	24
Tesco PLC	TSCO	1.68	373.50/.75	0.07	24
Nikkei 225	NIK	1.42	16230/40	0.06	24
USD/AUD - Australian $ per US$	USDAUD	0.69	0.7685/87	0.03	23
ARM Holdings PLC	ARM	4.58	114.50/.75	0.22	21
Autonomy Corporation PLC	AU.	4.75	408/09	0.24	20
BP PLC	BP.	1.63	598.00/.50	0.08	20
PartyGaming PLC	PRTY	4.25	115.25/.50	0.22	19
GBP/EUR - Euros per £	GBPEUR	0.45	0.6788/90	0.03	15
Land Securities Group PLC	LAND	1.27	1906.75/08.50	0.09	14
Regus Group PLC	RGU	6.17	102.75/03.25	0.48	13
Sage Group (The) PLC	SGE	2.75	242.50/43.00	0.21	13
Gold (LBM) $	G$	1.05	635.2/35.8	0.09	12
Vodafone Group PLC	VOD	2.39	114.50/75	0.22	11
FTSE Fixed Line Telecommunications	NMX6530	2.21	3082/90	0.26	9
FTSE 350 Construction & Materials	NMX2350	1.09	4316/26	0.23	5
Silver (LBM) $	S$	1.78	12.98/13.05	0.54	3

Source: ShareScope data

Bear in mind this is just a snapshot at one time, based on one firm's prices.

Nevertheless, there are some interesting points when we look at the figures.

- **Indices** score well here despite having lower volatility, because the spreads are so low. They might not move as fast as other instruments but it costs us less to get in and out of them. For that reason they are of particular interest to spread bettors just starting out.

- At the other end of the scale, the **sector** bets and **precious metal** bets with the firm that supplied the quotes do not look so attractive – the spreads are wide in comparison with the volatility.

- **Stocks** vary widely – interestingly the perennial favourite, Vodafone, is towards the bottom end of the table, spread bettors might be better off with a stock with greater volatility or a less expensive spread.

- **Currencies** are somewhere in the middle.

Differences between the spread betting firms

There is much common ground between the firms as to what you can bet on.

They will all do indices. Almost all will do the main commodities, FTSE 100 stocks and major currencies.

Then there also some differences. Some are keener than others on the smaller instruments. Occasionally we have seen an innovative instrument, such as the IG Index housing market bets, where you have been able to bet on the movement of house prices. And, as we have seen, most firms are happy to discuss potential bets with you even if they are not on the official menu.

Note: with the market evolving continually, information on specific spread betting firms may date quickly. If there is something you want to bet on, or something you want to know about the firms, you should check with the firms what their latest product offerings are. The quality of information on the web sites is in general very good.

Summary

I am perfectly happy to bet on indices, UK stocks, overseas stocks, commodities, interest rates or currencies. A fairly high proportion of my bets happen to have been on FTSE 100 and FTSE 250 stocks, but then I tend to follow these quite closely for other reasons such as investing in ISAs and SIPPs. Some people are more comfortable with the currencies, others with indices.

It really doesn't matter which you focus on, provided you are comfortable with the instruments you are dealing with; and that they have the three essential qualities of relatively:

1. high volatility,

2. good liquidity, and

3. small spreads.

Postscript

We now have a spread bet account, a computer and various other resources; we have an awareness of the types of instrument we can bet on and some of the key things winning spread bettors are looking for when deciding what to bet on.

We next need to look at the different types of spread bet on the market.

5

Choosing A Spread
Betting Type

This chapter runs through the various types of bets available in the market.

Let's assume we know what we want to bet on – we have decided that we want to place a bet on the FTSE100 stock BT Group PLC. There are still more choices to be made. There are at least five different instruments we can select to make bets on BT.

1. futures style

2. daily

3. rolling daily

4. binary

5. betting exchange

Note: these last two instruments are not strictly spread bets, but are mentioned en passant. These are discussed in more detail below.

Types of betting

1. Futures style

This is where spread betting started.

Futures style bets usually expire on a quarterly basis (March, June, September and December) and there are usually up to two quarters open at any point in time – the *near quarter* (expiring in 0 to 3 months) and the *far quarter* (expiring in 3 to 6 months). Note, not all firms offer the far quarter. But some offer quarters even further out. For example, if the date is 3 January, most firms will quote prices for contracts expiring in March and June, and some may even quote for September and December.

The pricing of the spread bet is based on the underlying futures price which will rarely be the same as the spot price because of the *cost of carry*. (For more information on cost of carry see: http://en.wikipedia.org/wiki/Cost_of_carry). If the spread bet was not based on the futures price there would be an arbitrage opportunity.

So, the spread bet price reflects a number of factors -

1. The current price of the instrument in the cash market or its equivalent.

2. Risk-free interest rate.

3. Yield. In the case of some instruments (e.g. commodities) there is no yield. In the case of stocks this would be dividends (adjustments up or down for any dividends in the period to expiry – down for longs and up for shorts). Effectively, if you are going long of a stock you can enter your bet more cheaply if dividends are due in the period as you are receiving the benefit of the dividends up front; and vice versa if you are going short.

4. Spreads in the underlying futures market (if there is one).

5. Additional spreads imposed by the spread betting firm.

At expiry, the futures premium (reflecting the cost of carry) will have converged to zero, and so the futures price (and spread price) will converge to the spot price.

> ### Example
>
> BT Group PLC is currently trading in the cash market at 248.75/249.00. We have about two weeks to go to the next futures expiry day, and the futures style spread bet is currently priced at 248.75/249.75. So, if we go long now there is an extra 0.75p built into the futures style spread bet.
>
> *What does that represent?*
>
> There are no dividends due in the period, so it represents interest costs. It is about 0.3% of the price. If you convert that into an annual interest rate it is about 7%.

2. Daily

Daily bets are straightforward. They are based on the cash market, or its equivalent, and expire at the end of the day.

With the cash market for BT Group PLC at 248.75/249.00 I have just tested the pricing with one of my spread betting accounts and got a quote for 248.75/249.00. That is what we want, no additional spread imposed on these types of bets by our spread betting firm. Bear in mind that this (good) situation will usually only arise with the most popular instruments (e.g. FTSE 100 stocks) and with the spread betting firms who are most competitive on pricing.

3. Rolling daily

Since their introduction a few years back, rolling daily bets have increased in popularity to the extent that they are now the preferred vehicle for a large number of spread bettors. They are based on the cash market or its equivalent, but instead of expiring at the end of the day like daily bets, they automatically roll over to the next day.

Compared with futures style bets the pricing is much easier to comprehend – it is the cash market adjusted for any additional spread the spread betting firm is adding, and you can see exactly what that price is if you have access to real time cash market data.

The elements of interest and dividends, instead of being incorporated into the price up front (as with futures style bets), are dealt with on a day by day basis in the following way-

Long positions

- *Interest you pay*: the closing price of the instrument is adjusted upwards each day by a factor based on the overnight interest rate plus 2 to 3% (varies by firm).

- *Dividends you receive*: the closing price of the instrument is adjusted downwards overnight to reflect the amount of the dividend per share.

Short positions

- *Interest you receive*: the closing price of the instrument is adjusted upwards each day by a factor based on the overnight interest rate less 2 to 3% (varies by firm).

- *Dividends you pay*: the closing price of the instrument is adjusted downwards overnight to reflect the amount of the dividend per share.

So, effectively you are paying overnight interest plus 2 to 3 % on longs, receiving overnight interest less 2 to 3 % on shorts, and either receiving or paying the full value of any dividends issued depending on whether you are long or short.

Example

Let's have a look at BT Group PLC again. With the cash market at 248.75/249.00 the quote for a rolling cash up bet was also at 248.75/249.00.

What happens if we open this bet at 249.00 and hold it open for a couple of weeks?

Each day we roll it over we pay an interest charge in the form of a financing adjustment. With the spread betting firm in question the financing charge on up bets is based on overnight interest rate plus 3%, which works out in this example at just over 7.8%.

Comparison with futures style bets

Not that different from the futures style spread bet, I hear you say. You are right for this two week timeframe.

Except for one critical difference.

If we decide to exit our bet, the spread on the rolling cash bet is only 0.25p, but the spread on the futures style bet is 1.00p. It is 4 times more expensive here to exit the futures style bet if we need to. This is the main reason why I prefer rolling daily bets.

4. Binary

In contrast to regular spread betting, binary bets at expiry only have two possible outcomes (hence the name). A positive outcome which is priced at 100, or a negative outcome which is priced at 0. Up until expiry the price of the bet will fluctuate according to the assessment of the spread betting firm, and the volume of business being received by the firm at various price levels.

Let's take an example of a binary bet which is for the FTSE 100 to close up on the day. Let's say that the FTSE is marginally up at lunch time. The price of this binary bet might at this point be 55-50. You think the FTSE will close up and you buy at one pound per point. This means that if you hold on to your bet until expiry and the FTSE does close up on the day your position will close at 100 (i.e. you will win £45: 100-55 x £1), but if the index ends down on the day your position will close 0 (i.e. a loss of £55: 0-55 x £1). With most firms you can close out your bet at any point in the day at a profit or a loss as the binary bet prices fluctuate.

Note: **It is worth pointing out that binary bets and fixed odds bets are not regulated by the FSA, whereas spread betting is.**

We will mention binary betting later in this book when we look at getting in and out of bets within a day. However, my preferred vehicle for most bets, and the main focus of this book, is financial spread betting.

5. Betting exchange

In recent years a new way to bet has developed. Betting exchanges have been formed which effectively allow you to make bets directly with other punters – eliminating the need for a spread betting firm to make the prices for you. These exchanges are particularly popular for sports betting, where there are strong views but also often a high degree of uncertainty or disagreement as to the basic facts such as which football team has the best players or which golfer is playing best at the moment. At the time of writing, while exchange betting is becoming increasingly popular for sports betting, it hasn't yet caught on in the same way for financial betting. For that reason I don't spend much time on this form of betting in this book, however there is a brief discussion of the subject in the appendix.

Differences between the spread betting firms

At the time of writing, between a third and a half of the firms have added binary (fixed odds) betting to their product list. All provide the futures style spread bets. Over half offer rolling daily bets.

It is likely that these differences will become smaller in the fairly near future. Firms will not be able to ignore the popularity of the rolling daily bet products, and more firms can be expected to enter the binary betting arena.

Postscript

We now have a spread betting account and appropriate resources to operate it, we know the range of instruments available to bet on and the types of bet available in the market.

But what timescales do spread bettors operate on?

The next chapter explores this issue.

6

Timescales For Spread Bets

This chapter explores the timescales used for spread betting. Spread bettors usually have one timescale that they feel most at home in. If you know your own mind on this issue, you might prefer to speed read the chapter.

The categorisation of timescales here is subjective but I have divided it into the following–

1. extremely short timescale

2. short timescale

3. medium timescale

4. long timescale

5. very long timescale

We shall now look at these in more detail below.

1. Extremely short timescale

This is defined as less than a day – we make a bet and close it the same day. For this timescale the daily bet product is an obvious choice, as is the binary bet. The most popular underlying instruments here tend to be indices or the most volatile stocks.

In Part 2 we look at a number of strategies specifically for this timeframe, looking at UK stocks. For some spread bettors this timescale will be too short. On this timescale we need quick reactions, precision timing and excellent discipline to be successful; we need to be able to exit slickly when things don't go in our favour. We also need real time data, a large account (to absorb the costs of the data) and a large amount of time available each day to monitor our trades.

2. Short timescale

This is defined as one to three days – typically we make a bet and close it out by the weekend. For this timescale the rolling daily bet is the obvious choice. Again, for many spread bettors this is a little on the short side.

3. Medium timescale

This is defined as a few days to a few weeks – typically three to thirty trading days. This is a popular timescale for spread betting with rolling daily bets. We make a bet, protecting it with a stop loss, then give it a little time to come good. Once the instrument has made a move, and loses momentum, we exit the bet and look for more promising material elsewhere.

This is really the heartland of spread betting, and from my perspective accounts for over 75% of all my bets.

4. Long timescale

This is defined as thirty days to three months. This is where the futures style spread bets come more into their own. If we know we want to keep a bet open for three months (we expect a persistent trend, or we need to give our bet a lot of time to come good), then the futures style spread bets work out a little cheaper than the rolling cash bets in total cost of carry. This is because they use base rate in the cost of carry calculations rather than the higher overnight rates of interest. However, if we need to exit early, they are much more expensive than rolling daily bets due to the much wider spreads.

> **Example: rolling v futures-style comparison**
>
> The two tables show various scenarios betting on ARM Holdings PLC with the underlying price remaining constant at 114p. In each scenario in the first table an up bet is placed just after the quarterly expiry. The illustrative prices were taken using the best prices quoted from a sample of three firms. In each scenario in the second table a down bet is placed just after the quarterly expiry.

Table 6.1: Up bet – rolling v futures-style comparison

Scenario	Sell after one month	Sell after two months	Sell after three months
Rolling cash entry	114.25	114.25	114.25
Rolling cash cost of carry	0.72	1.44	2.18
Rolling cash exit	114.0	114.00	114.00
Rolling cash total costs	0.97	1.69	2.43
Futures style entry (cost of carry included)	116.00	116.00	116.00
Futures style exit	114.50	114.25	114.00
Futures style total costs	1.50	1.75	2.00
Rolling cash better or worse?	Better	Better	Worse
How much by?	0.53	0.06	0.43

Table 6.2: Down bet – rolling v futures-style comparison

Scenario	Cover after one month	Cover after two months	Cover after three months
Rolling cash entry	114.00	114.00	114.00
Rolling cash interest received on short position	0.16	0.32	0.48
Rolling cash exit	114.25	114.25	114.25
Rolling cash total costs / (profit)	0.09	(0.07)	(0.23)
Futures style entry	114.75	114.75	114.75
Futures style exit	115.50	115.00	114.00
Futures style total costs / (profit)	0.75	0.25	(0.75)
Rolling cash better or worse?	Better	Better	Worse
How much by?	0.66	0.32	0.52

One can repeat this sort of experiment many times, and of course the results will vary by firm and by instrument. A few important observations from the tables above:

1. If we know for certain we are going to hold right through to the next quarterly expiry it is better to use a futures style bet.

2. For bets held for one or two months it is better to use a rolling cash bet.

3. If our timeframe is up to three months it will probably work out cheaper to use rolling cash bets when we factor in the fact that around half of our bets will be losers which we will have to exit well before the three months is up.

4. Interestingly, even if our bet goes nowhere for three months we make a small profit on a down bet whichever type of bet we take out, due to interest received. However, that interest received is a lot worse than putting the money on deposit, so there will have been an opportunity cost for us. And the spread betting firm will still have made a profit out of us since the rate of interest they earn will be much higher than the rate they pay us.

5. The figures for rolling cash bets depend on getting good tight spreads – in this case just 0.25 at a 114.0 underlying price; this is available, but not from all firms.

5. Very long timescale

Defined as over three months.

In the past, this was not a very common way to use spread betting. However, there are a number of products on the market to cater for the longer term spread bettor. Six monthly futures-style spread bets are an obvious example, and one or two firms have products even further out than six months.

With these longer term products it might be possible to use spread betting as an alternative to holding an instrument in an online broking account, although this has yet to catch on.

Here are some possible scenarios.

Bear in mind that if we use a spread bet to gain exposure to an instrument we only need a small amount of margin, and the rest of our funds can earn interest in a savings account.

In these scenarios we will assume–

- long: ARM Holdings PLC
- time horizon: 1 year
- market price at purchase: 114p
- total exposure £10,000
- market price at sale: 130p
- premium for a quarterly bet with 1p for rollovers : 2p
- premium for a 6 monthly bet with 1.5p for rollovers : 3p
- net interest earned in a savings account : 3%

No doubt these assumptions, valid at the time of writing, will change over time.

Table 6.3: spread betting v direct share investment comparison

Scenario	Long via a quarterly futures-style spread bet, rolled over 3 times	Long via a six monthly futures-style spread bet, rolled over once	Purchase stock via online broker, no capital gains tax	Purchase stock via online broker, capital gains tax allowance already fully used
Purchase / bet opening	(10000)	(10000)	(10000)	(10000)
Spread on initial purchase	(175)	(263)	(15)	(15)
Commission on purchase	0	0	(12)	(12)
Stamp duty	0	0	(50)	(50)
Cost of rollovers	(263)	(131)	0	0
Sale / bet closure	11404	11404	11404	11404
Spread on sale	0	0	(15)	(15)
Commission on sale	0	0	(12)	(12)
Profit before tax	966	1010	1300	1300
Capital gains tax	0	0	0	(520)
Net interest earned via savings account	270	270	0	0
Profit after tax	1236	1280	1300	780

Spread betting – a long-term buy-and-hold instrument?

There are many assumptions in this analysis. The point is to draw attention to the misconception that spread betting is only short term. If we can use the leverage of spread betting and stick the balance of our funds in a savings account, plus get good spreads on our spread bets, it is possible to get close to the total return of investing in an online broking account on a before tax basis. And, needless to say, the post tax position is even better. This is not the way most people think about spread betting, but this may be an important development in the future.

Postscript

We now have an understanding of the timescales spread bettors operate on. But there are criticisms of spread betting – we need to tackle a number of these head on before we go any further.

7

Pricing And Hedging

This chapter tackles a range of controversial issues which have cropped up in the spread betting arena over the years.

Do they really want you to win?

This is a controversial subject – there are a couple of schools of thought–

1. The "they want you to win" argument: which not surprisingly, tends to be implied in the marketing literature of the spread betting firms, and is based on the notion that all spread bets are hedged by the firms – so if you win they don't lose, you're happy and you bet again.

2. The "they want you to lose" argument: which is based on the notion that the firms' profits have to come from somewhere and that is very probably *us* – the punters. Think casinos...

It is worth stepping back for a moment and looking at the business model of a spread betting firm. It is clearly a good model – there is no doubt that a good spread betting firm can be very profitable. A quick glance at the public figures released by quoted spread betting firms shows they are cash machines.

Let's look at the various sources of profit.

Interest

First up, interest. As an example, let's take the popular rolling daily bet. And let's assume the rate charged on long positions is the overnight rate plus 3%, and the rate given on shorts is the overnight rate minus 3%. Let's assume an overnight market rate of 4.75%, and that the firm's credit standing allows it to borrow and lend at that rate. Let's also assume that all bets are hedged and that if the customer is long the firm also has to go long and has to borrow at the overnight rate to fund the purchase of the hedging instrument, or go short if the customer is short.

This is looking very attractive from the viewpoint of the spread betting firms.

- if the customers are **long**, the firms lend money at 7.75% and borrow at 4.75%

- if the customers are **short**, the firms pay out interest at 1.75% and get paid at 4.75%.

Admittedly there are transaction costs to consider, and actual interest rates will differ slightly, but one could build a successful banking business with figures like that!

Spreads

Next, spreads. The firms for the most part add an additional spread on to the market spread. And, with their purchasing power in the market, they will be able to trade well within the market spread when they need to hedge. The online stock broking firms can make money by charging a small commission, then giving the customer a price just inside the market spread. So it should be easy to make money just from the spreads, if the spread betting firms trade within the spread but charge their customers outside it.

Hedging and position taking

Finally, hedging and position taking. If, for a spread betting firm, half the customers are long an instrument and half the customers are short the instrument, they don't need to hedge. The profit for the winning customers will be paid by the losing customers, and the spread betting firm will make money from the spread and from the interest.

If the spread betting book is not balanced and the customers have a net long or short position, the spread betting firm can hedge the net position. Or, if they are confident in their trading skills and believe their customers are wrong in their net position, they can take the decision not to hedge. In this case, if things go as they expect, they will win, while on a net basis their customers will lose. Each and every day they monitor their customers' net positions and decide whether to hedge or to trade against them. If they have a skilled trading team the trading team will be a major source of profits in its own right.

Add all this together and you get a seriously impressive profit-making machine.

From a personal viewpoint, I have absolutely no problem whatsoever if a spread betting firm decides to take a view and not hedge its customers' positions (i.e. take a trading position on them).

If it does this, so what?

It doesn't affect whether I personally win or not. And that's what matters to me. On the other hand, I am concerned about the interest rate I pay on longs or get on shorts and about the size of the spreads; because that does affect me.

As a customer I want the spread betting firms to make money. Because this is such a profitable market for the spread betting firms there is competition amongst them for our business. Which means in the longer run tighter spreads and better rates of interest, as customers become more sophisticated and more prone to switch to a more generous firm. The firms will continue to make good profits but the winning spread bettors will find they have made a little more out of their spread betting at the end of the year.

How spread betting firms work out their prices

The relevant questions to ask here are–

* Is there an underlying market?

* How transparent is it?

If there is an underlying market, then all the firms will have the same start point. And if it is transparent then not only all the firms, but also all the customers, will potentially be able to know where the underlying market is trading.

Price based on the underlying market

Take a simple example: a daily bet on a UK stock. The UK stock will be trading in the underlying market, with a known spread. The firms' quotes for bets on this stock will in general be directly linked to the spread in the underlying market. At the time of writing most of them will be adding a small percentage to the offer and subtracting a small percentage from the bid (i.e. creating a wider spread), but the quotes will in principle move in line with the underlying market. There are however some differences between the firms in the speed with which their betting quotes react to changes in the underlying market, the fastest being just a fraction of a second.

Reality may be different from the official prices

However, in practice it is a little more complicated than this.

Sometimes the spread for an instrument in the underlying market is misleading in that the order book is tiny for the spread quoted, and in practice if you were to deal in the underlying market you would get worse prices. And **the firms' quotes for bets on the instrument reflect the reality rather than the official bid/offer spread in the underlying market.** Sometimes the spread betting firms will have preferred market makers with whom they hedge, and will use those market makers' spreads as a base for their quotes for bets. These spreads may differ slightly from the official bid/offer spread in the underlying market.

Are spread prices ever skewed?

A concern with many spread bettors is whether the firms skew their prices in line with market trends – adding to the offer price when the customers are going long and lowering the bid when they are going short.

This is particularly worrying if you are trying to exit in a hurry. **The bad news is that, if you read the small print, most spread betting firms are entitled to change their spreads as they see fit.** Just as a bookie shortens or lengthens the odds as the punters place their bets. The better news is that, with increased competition amongst the spread betting firms, and increased sophistication amongst the customers, in today's market a firm would have to be very careful about adopting such tactics as a matter of routine. If word got out customers would be quickly moving their business elsewhere. With rolling daily bets it is obvious when a spread betting firm's prices get out of line with the market. Sharp day traders would have the opportunity to take advantage of the skewed prices to take trades in the opposite direction.

The solution, as is often the case with spread betting, is to have more than one account to retain flexibility. Be prepared to vote with your feet.

If there is no underlying market

Where there is no underlying market, then the firms will have to provide their quotes using skill.

Take the example of a binary bet on the position of the FTSE 100 at 12 noon today. Although the bet is clearly based on the FTSE 100 and we can all know where it is trading right this second (let's say it's 11 a.m. now) there is no underlying instrument for a 12 noon FTSE 100. So the spread betting firm will have to set the quotes for the binary bet using whatever parameters they believe are appropriate. They might move their bid and ask prices during the next hour based not only on how the FTSE moves but also on how the customers bet. That's just like a bookie. That's also what happens on a betting exchange, where you can get to play the bookie.

Futures style bets

The prices of futures style bets have on occasion caused great confusion to customers. The basic approach is as follows-

1. If there is an underlying futures contract for the period (e.g. an oil future) then the spread betting firm will probably base its quotes for bets on the price of the underlying futures contract.

2. For a financial instrument (e.g. a stock) that has no related futures contract in the underlying market, then the price will be based on the forward price. This is the current cash price of the stock adjusted for dividends in the period (if any) and interest (using a standard approach to pricing futures contracts). For example, for an up bet, the formula is Current cash price - Dividends to be received in the period + Interest. In effect, with an up bet you get the benefit of the dividend you would be due in the period up front (i.e. it is built in to the price you pay to gain exposure to the stock), but you also have to pay interest, reflecting the fact that you are not paying for the stock in full up front.

As transparency declines

As transparency declines, inevitably there is greater opportunity for the spread betting firm to run their portfolio more like a traditional bookie.

For instance, let's take a small cap stock where there is no futures contract, that is currently trading in the underlying market at 500-502. The calculations for cost of carry (add interest subtract dividends for a long, vice versa for a short) come to say 10p, and with a wider spread the firm initially quotes 510-514p. And many customers decide to go long. The firm will probably just hedge here (buy the appropriate amount of the underlying instrument), but certainly in the past they might also have widened the spread so new up bets would become more expensive. Let's say to 510-520p.

Repeating an earlier point, it is a good idea to have more one than account – so you can compare quotes between the firms.

How competitive is the market?

The answer is: increasingly so. It is a standard principle of economics that lucrative industries with relatively low barriers to entry will attract new entrants – which is exactly what we have seen in the case of spread betting.

Competition amongst the spread betting firms in the last few years in particular has produced noticeable improvements for their customers, such as–

1. reduced spreads,

2. much improved trading platforms,

3. new popular features introduced by one firm are soon copied by the others (e.g. rolling daily bets), and

4. improved quality of service.

As an example of how the spreads have improved let's look at a simple example of the FTSE 100.

Nowadays the firms with the best spreads are able to quote a 2 point spread for a daily or rolling cash bet. For instance, our volatility table earlier showed the bet quoted at 5958-60. After hours the spread widens to say 4 points. Futures style bets for this instrument have a 5 point spread for the near quarter (as I write this it is 2 weeks away – earlier in the quarter the spread was 6 points).

Contrast this with a few years ago when the first firm reduced its spread to 6 and the pack were at 8 to 10.

This reduction in spreads has not been confined to indices – stocks and foreign exchange spreads in particular have also benefited.

Do they hedge?

We looked at the concept of spread betting firms hedging or not hedging their customers bets when we looked at their business model. We saw that it was possible for a spread betting firm to make profits (or losses) by keeping at least a portion of the customers book unhedged.

But what actually happens in real life – do they hedge or don't they?

The answer is: yes and no.

Some spread bettors have a naïve view that as soon as they place an up bet on Vodafone at £20 per point, the spread betting firm is going to rush out and buy a two and a half grand CFD to hedge the position. But put yourself in the position of the spread betting firm. About 10 seconds later someone who has the opposite view as you will be placing a down bet on Vodafone. So why hedge?

There are three obvious factors for the spread betting firm to consider in the decision whether to hedge or not:

1. Size

Basic cost/benefit analysis suggests that for small bets the costs of hedging will be greater than the probable risk in running with the small exposure on your bet.

2. Overall net position of customers

It is common sense that the firm will want to hedge the *net position* on a rolling basis, rather than hedge each bet individually; risk management is a highly skilled endeavour, and a good risk manager will look not only at the net long or short position on individual instruments but also at the correlation between instruments; one could manage exposure at a sector level for instance rather than at an individual stock level, to take one very simple example.

3. Risk view

Whether the firm is going to take a position on an instrument, by not hedging. I will repeat that I have no problem at all if the firm does this, they are taking a view on the market which doesn't affect my position.

So yes, they do hedge, but not as much as everyone thinks.

Future developments – a wish list

A very simple wish list–

1. Better spreads please, and more generous terms on interest.

2. I will switch business to the first firm to offer guaranteed yellow strip on rolling daily bets (no rollover commission, no re-quotes) and Libor plus 0.2% or minus 0.4%.

Thanks

Postscript

We have been travelling some while and have just crossed some difficult terrain on our way to Base Camp. We have a spread bet account, a computer and appropriate additional resources. We know what we can bet on and the types of bet available in the market place. We are also aware of some of the controversial issues which have cropped up in the spread betting arena over the years.

But what about our fellow spread bettors? Are they all winning? Is there a load of easy money to be made now?

If you are taking the trouble to read this book you probably already know the answers to those questions; quite a few spread bettors stumble as they start to climb the mountain. It is worth taking a look at some of the more common ways they go wrong.

8

10 Common And Really Expensive Spread Betting Errors

In this chapter we look at ten common and expensive errors people make spread betting and at ways to avoid them.

1. No edge

An easy way to lose money fast is to spread bet without an edge.

What's your edge?

Don't know? If you don't know what your edge is then it is highly probable you haven't got one. And if you haven't got one you probably aren't going to win.

An edge at spread betting is a methodology which if repeated over time can be expected to net you a profit. For example by generating either a high frequency of wins, or a high ratio of average win size to average loss size, or a combination of the two.

We look at a range of strategies which can give you an edge during the course of this book. It is worth pointing out at this early stage that you can get an edge from a variety of sources – superior entries, superior exits, superior money or risk management. You can even get an edge by knowing when to stand aside and not bet at all. Overall, the most durable edges will have a little of all of these.

There are two good ways of proving to yourself that you have an edge–

1. Can you explain your edge by writing it down?

2. Can you measure it?

This requires planning... [Of which, more later.]

2. No planning

Which leads us on to another source of failure at spread betting: having no plan.

It is often quite a surprise for the beginner to learn how much planning more successful spread bettors actually do. Plans come in many shapes and sizes. Winners often have some sort of annual plan, plus a detailed short-term plan (e.g. a game plan for the next week), plus detailed trade plans for the next day, as well as written details of their trading methodology and rules.

A common symptom of someone having a go at spread betting lacking adequate plans is that they become heavily reliant on tips. Since they have not worked out their own method of determining which bets to take, they eagerly drink in tips from the weekly magazines, television, daily papers, bulletin boards, web sites, newsletters, work colleagues, friends, or anyone they meet who happens to have a tip. There is absolutely no shortage of tips for those who want them. Trouble is, most tips providers don't have a record much better than 50%, and with some you are actually better off taking the other side of their trade recommendations.

And most tips only suggest an entry – what about the exit, money management, and risk management?

If you are at the stage where you trade primarily on other people's tips, chances are you are not winning.

3. Wrong bet size

You might think that if you know when to enter a bet and when to exit it, you are there. Far from it! Since you will have losing as well as winning bets, it is absolutely essential to get the size of your bets right.

Case Study 1

Paul is a hardworking salesperson who has only fairly recently set up an account with a spread betting firm. He has £2000 in his account, and has just about got the hang of using the spread betting firm's trading software. He has recently become bullish on the mining stock BHP Billiton and has decided to place an up bet on it. The stock is currently trading at 1070p, and Paul opens the bet online first thing in the morning at 1070.25p for £50 per point. He reckons the stock should get up to 1100p, which will net him about £1500.

After an exceptionally busy day at work, when he next goes online at 4.00pm to see how much money he has made. Unfortunately, all the mining stocks have had a bad day and BHP Billiton is down 14.25p at 1056p (bid price) – he has lost £712.50.

He receives an email from his spread betting firm explaining that he needs to put more money into his account if he wants to keep his bet open. He has lost just over 35% of his £2000 spread betting funds in one day. Paul decides to cut his losses at this stage, and closes the bet.

Over the next 6 trading days BHP Billiton does indeed reach 1100p as Paul had hoped, but he has lost money on the bet.

What went wrong?

Paul didn't work out in advance the point at which he would decide his bet was wrong, in fact he only considered the upside. Spread betting is a percentage game, and you always need to consider the downside before you place a bet. Just as importantly, Paul's size of bet was ludicrous in relation to his account size. It is always a good idea to work out what your bet is equivalent to if you were buying or selling the instrument outright. Multiply £50 by 1070.25p, and we see that Paul bought the equivalent of £53,512.50 of BHP Billiton stock − over 26 times his account size.

We look at bet sizing in some detail in this book, but a good rule of thumb is that the amount you lose if you are wrong shouldn't exceed 2% of your account. In Paul's case, he should have decided in advance that he would get out of the bet at a certain point if it went against him − let's say that he decided that point was 1045p. That's an adverse move of 25.25p. 2% of his account would be £40, and to keep the loss on an adverse move to £40 or less he could in fact only afford £1 per point on this bet.

This case study is a good example of a phenomenon called overtrading. Overtrading comes in several shapes and forms and often results in the destruction of an account. In this case it was one bet that was way too big for the account. Overtrading also occurs when the total number of open bets is too big for the account. And when the frequency of bets is too high for the account.

4. No risk management

In Case Study 1 we see an example of betting with no exit plan in place. This is a recipe for losing money fast. **Before any bet is made you need to decide where you will enter the bet, where you will get out at a loss, how much to bet and where your initial profit target will be.**

In this game you have to play good defence, and manage the downside as well as you manage the upside. The sad reality is that many people go into spread betting expecting easy money and focus almost exclusively on the upside. Then they mismanage the downside, suffer a few horrendous losses and eventually give up. Risk management entails having clear exit points for all your bets so no individual loss can get out of control; it also entails keeping your total exposure under control. To win at this game this is essential.

5. Mistiming exits

It is a common belief that winning at spread betting is mainly about entering bets well. So if one could just find a better system for making bets (for example, the diligent search for the elusive ten-baggers), one could win more. Many people spend money on books and on courses to improve their bet placing.

In practice the reality for most people is that they could make a far bigger difference to their overall performance if they spent an equivalent amount of effort on improving the timing of their exits.

Case Study 2

Sally has had a spread betting account for more than a year and has made a reasonable start at it. She works as a computer programmer and although she has a demanding job she is able to monitor her bets at fairly regular intervals during the day. Jane is an accounts clerk who has several spread betting accounts and is now making almost as much out of spread betting as she does from her accounts job.

They both enter the same two bets on 8 Feb 2006: short Rank at 265p (£19 per point) and short Morrison at 187p (£26 per point), with the equivalent of approximately £5000 on each bet.

Jane places automated stop losses on the 2 trades at 277p and 193p respectively; and has initial profit targets for both bets at a ratio of 2:1 to her risk, i.e. at 241p for Rank (265 – (2 x 277-265)) and 175p for Morrison (187 – (2 x 193-187)).

Sally prefers to monitor her bets during the day without an automated stop, but agrees that 277p and 193p are indeed about the right levels for stops.

The Rank bet doesn't do too well initially: at one point getting up to 276p, but not enough to trigger Jane's stop or to cause Sally to get out. On the 14th trading day of the bet they find they are breakeven for the first time at one point in the day, and on the 15th trading day the bet goes slightly into profit. Sally decides it's time to exit and covers near the close at 260.5p producing a profit of £85.50 (19 x (265-260.5)). For

---

Jane nothing has happened yet to prompt her to close the bet. Rank declines over the next 3 days, and on this last day there is an increase in volume combined with a late recovery in the stock which suggests to Jane its time to bank profits, which have achieved her target. She covers at 238p producing a profit of £513 (19 x (265-238)).

The Morrison bet is no good at all.

Jane's automated stop is hit on day 4 and she is out for a loss of £156 (26 x (193-187)). She has no problem with this – some you win and some you lose, so best keep the losses small and the wins big. £357 up overall on her 2 bets.

Sally on the other hand is in trouble. She didn't exit the Morrison bet when it hit 193p and then watches anxiously as it touches 199p five days later and finally gaps up to 204p the next day on big volume. She gets out at 205.5p for a loss of £481 (26 x (205.5-187)). Overall loss on her two bets £395.50.

Same two bets, yet one person wins well, the other loses. One took a big win and a small loss, the other took a small win and a big loss. Day in day out, this happens all the time with spread bettors, and the long term winners are the ones who can exit losers promptly and run their winners.

There are two costs to holding on to losers as Sally did. Obviously you lose money; but you also lose confidence and this has a knock on effect on your subsequent performance.

What's worse than hanging on too long to a loser? Adding to it. You won't win if you keep on adding to your losers. For example, you bought Vodafone at 130p and it's down to 122p, so you want to buy more because it's even cheaper?

Wrong!

You're thinking like a value investor – not a trader. If it's not showing a profit, don't add to it.

In a similar vein, if you decide it's time to cut back on your exposure, and you have three bets, two winners and one loser, most people will cash in one of the winners and hope the loser will "come good". Far better to get rid of the loser, and see if the winners do even better.

6. Out of control

When we place a bet, it might win, it might lose, or it might break even. There is no way we can know which of these outcomes will materialise at the time we make the bet. If we have an edge, over the long run our betting will have a positive expectancy, but any one bet could be a loser. We play the odds, try to avoid errors, and let our edge play itself out. It's very similar to playing poker.

Does this mean we are just buying a lottery ticket and hoping for the best?

Far from it, and we need to control everything that can be controlled throughout the game of spread betting. Losers tend not to be in control (as can be seen in Case Study 3).

Case Study 3

John, who works in advertising, had a few initial successes when he opened a spread betting account seven months ago, but for the last few months it's been mainly downhill. He wants some advice. I look at his current trades, and to get the conversation going, ask him why he is long the dollar. "Long?" he queries, with a puzzled look, "I am short the dollar, it's going down". I show him the statement and he looks shocked. He tends to phone in his bets rather than using the online facilities, and it is becoming clear he called this one in the wrong way round. This was more than a week ago, he never checked the statement, and if it was the spread betting firm's mistake it's getting pretty late to try and sort it. He calls the firm, they go back to their tapes and it eventually emerges he did call it in the wrong way round. Better get out of that one then.

I follow up by asking him why he is long Rexam, it has been a good bet for the last couple of weeks, but he has no record and no immediate recollection of why he entered the bet. Then he remembers, he likes to use a number of indicators including stochastics and RSI and they both appeared oversold at the time. Does he have a profit target or a stop on the Rexam bet? Well, sort of, but it's not written down anywhere, and seems to involve a bit of gut feel.

What about a trade plan for today? Nothing official, but oil has pulled back to a support level around $60 and he reckons it should be back on its way higher soon.

What will specifically trigger this trade?

No answer. John gets an urgent call and we agree to get going again in half an hour. When we regroup I discover that John has in the interim called in an up bet on oil. Same question as before: what specific trigger is there for this trade? "It has to go up" he asserts, with some confidence. I ask him how much margin he has now in his account, he can't tell me. He repeats his views on oil.

No planning, no monitoring of the account, no real methodology for entries or exits, too much reliance on gut feel. All basic errors, no real control. John has got to get back to basics before he has got any chance of winning in the long run.

7. Not in tune with the markets

Sometime in early 2002, when the bear market in stocks was well underway, I was attending a conference and got talking with an analyst with one of the spread betting firms. He mentioned that over 90% of his customers were still long. About 8 or 9 months later I met him again at another conference, and the news was his customers were still well over 50% long. Many of them would have been nursing big losses. They were no doubt just getting the hang of the short side when a new bull market started in March 2003.

There are studies going back to the 1930s which show that most people have a bias to the long side. It may sound obvious, but if the market is going down we want to be mainly short, and if it's going up we want to be mainly long. **Many spread bettors lost money from 2001 to early 2003 because they didn't adjust their approach to stay in tune with the overall stock market direction, which was obviously down.**

8. Running before walking

If someone came up to you and said they were taking a course in dentistry over the weekend and setting up as a dentist next week, you wouldn't believe them, and you certainly wouldn't want them anywhere near your teeth. But plenty of people come into spread betting expecting to be able to pick it up over a weekend and start winning straightaway. Perhaps you are thinking, there is no comparison, it takes years of learning and practice to become a dentist, whereas spread betting is easy.

The reality is that while it doesn't take nearly as long as becoming a dentist, it does take time to learn to win consistently at spread betting. You have to develop an edge that is right for you and then you have to learn how to use it with real money. If you try to run before you can walk you can lose a lot of money very fast. There have been a number of estimates made by writers and journalists on how many people win overall at spread betting in their first year; the figure is almost certainly a lot less than 50%, and probably quite a bit less than 25%, with some people even suggesting a figure below 10%. That is because you can get nearly everything right and still lose if you get one major thing wrong such as bet size or risk management.

It is best to assume that it will take a good year to become proficient at spread betting, and to keep bet sizes low while in learning mode. There is no substitute for experience and practice, and in the end the real teacher is always the market itself.

9. Emotionally unstable

Some people are just not cut out for spread betting. It can be a rough ride at times. In my day job I can have a bad day and I still get paid. In spread betting I can have a bad day and I might lose more than I earn in a day in my day job. What is worse, I might have done nothing wrong either. My entries were well thought through and executed exactly as planned, stops all in the right place, bet size right, everything done according to the book; but the market moves against me and I lose.

This comes with the territory I am afraid. If this is going to upset you, then spread betting might not be for you. If you have an edge you will win in the long run, but you will have to endure some losing periods (draw downs) as sure as night follows day. You need emotional stability to get through that. People without that stability are going to find the game too stressful. There is an old saying:

scared money can't win

Note: If you are a gambler by nature, then be very wary of spread betting. If you find that getting the adrenalin rush from placing a bet is more important to you than winning, you should stay well away from spread betting. Winners get their kicks outside spread betting, they are playing the game to win.

Equally, you have to be able to take the rough with the smooth. You are going to get both in spread betting. If you get a big high from your wins and get depressed when you have a loss you are going to be on a permanent emotional roller coaster, and spread betting is going to mess you up.

10. Not taking responsibility

For many people it is very hard to accept full responsibility for their spread betting results. All sorts of excuses come out for losses. A common scapegoat is the spread betting firm itself: maybe the spread was a bit wider than usual, or there was some slippage on the automated stop. Or maybe an article that became the basis of a bet was a bit misleading. Or a book on trading that we have been reading hasn't been producing the results we expected. Or a tip we have used hasn't worked out. Or we have had some bad luck. As long as the excuses keep pouring out we are running away from the real issue which is how to improve our spread betting performance.

Winning spread bettors tend to have a different attitude. They accept that whatever triggered their potential interest in a specific bet and whichever firm they used to make it, in the end the result they got was down to them. They are in control of their spread betting and fully responsible for its results.

Postscript

For the first time on our journey to Base Camp we have had a glimpse of the real danger we will face on the Mountain Spread Betting. It has just been brought home to us that people perish on the Mountain. In the next chapter we will look at an essential piece of safety equipment, the stop loss.

9

Keeping Losses Small – The Stop Loss

In this chapter we take a good look at the stop loss.

Cart before the horse?

We haven't even placed a bet yet, and here we are about to discuss one way of exiting them! But for many losing spread bettors the two following simple rules could improve their performance significantly–

- **Rule One**: Always determine *before* you place your bet the point at which you will exit the bet if it goes against you.

- **Rule Two**: See Rule One.

But there's no such thing as a free lunch. In spread betting there are often trade offs. Potential advantages are often partially offset by potential disadvantages. This is particularly noticeable as we look at the stop loss.

Stop or no stop?

Let's address the basic question here –

what is the purpose of stop losses?

Simply, their purpose is to...stop losses! To be more accurate, their purpose is to stop big losses, to limit the size of a loss to an amount which fits in with our approach to risk management.

You will occasionally read articles in investment magazines written by someone who is strongly opposed to setting stop losses; they might tell a story of how one of their investments dropped past the level a stop loss would have been at and then recovered nicely to earn them a bumper profit. You should ignore any suggestion of trading without stop losses for the following reasons:

1. You are probably not making *long term investments* with your spread bets. A value investor would often treat a drop in price as an opportunity to buy more. For instance, the legendary Warren Buffett probably doesn't use stop losses – *but he is not trading.*

2. For trading short term it is essential to place a cap on any one particular loss; if a bet is going against us more than a pre-defined amount we want to exit and redirect our spread betting funds to more promising areas. We don't have time to wait like a value investor for the instrument to turn around.

3. Spread betting is a leveraged product; this means losses as well as gains are multiplied. It is important therefore to keep them under control.

So, the stop loss is a predetermined point at which we will exit a bet. We can place an automated stop with our spread betting firm or we can track progress of our bet ourselves and take action when the stop loss point is reached. Whichever technique we use to implement the stop loss the basic rule is straightforward: for every bet we have open we must know the point at which we will close the bet because it is moving against us.

We use stop losses so that when we are wrong on our bet we take a manageable loss, preserving capital for the times we are right on our bets.

Two caveats on stop losses

1. Having an automated stop in place doesn't guarantee we will be able to exit at our stop price. If the market is moving fast we may suffer slippage (i.e. get a worse price than our stop price). This can happen for a variety of reasons; if everyone else is trying to exit at the same time the market will be moving fast and will move against us in the time between the point our stop is triggered and the point when our bet is actually closed. Or the price of the instrument may even gap right past our stop point (this can happen when markets gap open in the morning).

2. We should focus on establishing appropriate stop losses for our style of betting and implementing them properly. But even if we do this right, sometimes we will get stopped out of a bet, only to see later that the bet would have been successful if only we could have hung on a bit longer. That's one of the trade offs we mentioned.

Near or far?

Losing spread bettors focus too much on how to enter a bet rather than this essential decision of where to place the stop loss for best effect.

But how do we decide where to put stops?

We want to put them far enough away so that we don't get stopped out by random movements in the market; but near enough to keep our losses small when we are wrong. Too near, and we will take a lot of small losses and kill promising bets too early, too far away and our losses will be too big.

What are random movements?

It's worth pointing out here that the study of stop levels can be very complex; whole books could be written about just this. And there are many different ways of calculating optimised stop levels. We illustrate here a straightforward and practical method to keep the stop levels beyond random movements.

Let's take the example of a bet we expect to last two or three weeks. We can define random movements (or "noise") as the amount on average the instrument fluctuates each day. Let's take the example of the US index, the S&P500. My software calculates a figure called the Average True Range (ATR) for each instrument, which averages the range between the high and the low price of the day over a number of days set by the user. The ATR for the S&P500 is currently 12 and the index level is at 1294. Suppose we want to enter a down bet at 1294, expecting to keep it open for a couple of weeks. Our stop should be set at least 12 above 1294 (i.e. at least at 1306). More practical would be to use a multiple of the ATR, say 2, and set our stop 24 above i.e. at 1318.

The more volatile instruments have relatively high ATRs and therefore require stops further away in percentage terms than the less volatile instruments.

For example, ARM Holdings PLC currently has an ATR of just over 3, which is about 3% of the price; whereas the S&P ATR of 12 is only about 1% of the price.

Automated or mental?

If we automate our stop losses by programming them into our spread betting firm's trading platform we know they will be executed when the price reaches them; we will not be called upon to make a decision.

If we just make a mental note (or written, or typed) of the stop loss point, we will have some flexibility to manage our way out of the bet when the stop loss point has been reached; on the other hand we may mismanage this and get a worse price, or worse still, override our stop and reset it somewhere else.

It takes excellent personal discipline to use mental stops as opposed to automated stops. Best practice is to automate them provided you are dealing with liquid instruments. However be careful with automated stops on less liquid instruments – you may find you have been stopped out by a short term price aberration.

For example, with UK stocks I automate stops on FTSE100 stocks, currencies and indices and on the biggest 20 or 30 of the FTSE250 stocks. For smaller stocks I automate only if the distance from the stop is more than 2.5 times the average daily price range of the stock.

Instant or delayed?

Automated stops are executed instantly. If you have a mental stop, you have a further decision, whether to act on it instantly if it gets hit, or to manage your way out. Be very careful with trying to manage your way out, the mind plays all manner of tricks on people – especially at those times when things are going wrong.

In general, if you have done your research right and found the correct place to put your stop, according to your betting methodology, then when the stop point is reached, get out!

Techniques for placing stops

Technical analysis can also be useful for placing stops.

I will illustrate this with an example of a down bet on the FTSE100. The index closed at 5858 on 7 Sep (see chart below).

© ShareScope

During the following day a rally takes it up to 5898, which is when we decide we want to place a down bet.

Where would our stop loss go?

There are many different techniques for setting stops, including–

1. Average True Range

2. Support and resistance

3. Moving averages

4. Highest high or lowest low

5. Money stops

These five techniques are described in some detail below.

1. Average True Range

The chart shows the 10-day ATR at 54, so taking twice the ATR and adding it to the 7 September close our stop would go at 5966. If we used just one times the ATR it would be closer, at 5912. Our loss would be smaller if we got stopped out, on the other hand we would be more likely to get stopped out. Trade-offs!

2. Support and resistance

Support is where price stopped falling in the past, resistance is where it stopped rising. It is logical to put stops the other side of support (for an up bet) or resistance (for a down bet). Effectively we are treating the support or resistance point as a barrier. When price reaches the barrier we are expecting it to bounce off it and reverse direction. If the barrier is penetrated we take that as a significant warning sign and exit our bet. You can see on the chart that FTSE100 has turned down twice from just below 6000, so we could put our stop just above the thick black line representing resistance on the chart, say at 6010.

Support and resistance are referred to on several occasions in this text, and a brief further explanation of this important concept is included in the Appendix.

3. Moving averages

Moving averages can be used to place stops – we can for instance place a very tight stop just above the 10 day moving average (the wavy line on the chart). The average is currently at 5919 so we could place our stop at say 5930.

4. Highest high or lowest low

We can use the highest high of the last x days as a stop (for a down bet) or the lowest low (for an up bet). For instance we might decide that we want to exit our down bet if price moves above the highest high of the last 5 days. That is 5991, so our stop could go at 5992.

5. Money stops

Some people use money stops – they set their stop at a point which limits their loss to a certain amount of money. Some people argue against money stops, preferring to identify a logical place on the chart to put a stop first and then link the size of their bet to the stop point, rather than identifying the stop point directly from the bet size; but people who use money stops generally believe they work well. In this case, let us say we always bet £2 per point on the FTSE100 and always limit our loss to £200. That means we can risk 100 points from our entry point of 5898, so our stop would go at 5998.

Other techniques not illustrated here include using trend lines or indicators to signal an exit.

This table below summarises where our stop would go, by technique.

Type of stop	Stop level
Average true range x 2 / x 1	5966 / 5912
Resistance	6010
10 day moving average	5930
High of last 5 days	5992
Money stop	5998

We seem spoiled for choice. Different approaches suit different people.

My personal preference is to use a blend of techniques for setting stops. However, I usually give precedence to support and resistance on the chart and try to place my stops just beyond the support/resistance. So my stop on this down bet on the FTSE100 is at 6010. And it is automated in the spread betting firm's trading system. If buyers push the price up to there, beyond the resistance, it will be a clear sign that my down bet was a mistake. I will want to get out of the bet immediately – and since the stop is automated the system will do this for me without any manual intervention on my part.

One more useful approach – the time stop

Once we have decided on our stop loss, there is another discipline we can add to manage the bets that don't work out. The stop loss takes care of the bet that goes in the wrong direction for us, but what about the bet that goes nowhere? The solution here is a mental stop called the *time stop*.

Time stops are useful – we stipulate a certain period of time after which we scrub the bet if it hasn't gone into profit – the theory being that if a bet has gone nowhere after that period of time it is tying up betting funds that could be put to better use elsewhere.

> I use time stops. For instance if a bet has gone nowhere for a period of 10 days I get out.

Two tips

Tip #1

Whichever technique you decide to use it is best not to place stops exactly where everyone else has also placed them. Market makers love to push the price just beyond where (they know) all the stops are and then back again, making a quick profit as all the stops are triggered. Avoid:

* round numbers such as 500, 6000; and

* the exact level of a very obvious support/resistance level.

In both these cases, put the stop just a little bit further away e.g. 503, 6030, or an extra 0.5% beyond the support/resistance.

Tip #2

Know what triggers a stop with your spread betting firm; some use actual market prices, some use their own prices, some use the bid or ask price rather than the market price. Some offer you a choice, I always use the underlying market price if possible.

Moving stops

Once you have set your stop loss, when – if ever – do you move it?

The rules here are simple.

Rule 1

If the bet goes against you, *never* move the stop further away from your entry position.

Typical scenario for the losing spread bettor – take the example of the FTSE100 down bet we looked at above. Stop set at 6002. Price moves to 5999.

First thought: "My stop is about to get hit."

Second thought: "It's a good trade really."

Third thought: "Let's move the stop to 6020."

Fourth thought (a few days later after the stop has been moved, then eventually hit at 6020): "This isn't a good bet after all, I really wish I had got out earlier."

Result: a bigger loss.

Rule 2

If the bet moves in your favour then you can start moving the stop nearer to the current price.

This is called *trailing* the stop (or *using a trailing stop loss*). It is a valuable tool for the spread bettor. We will have more to say on the trailing stop loss in Part Two.

At this stage let's look at how one can trail a stop loss using each of the five techniques above.

1. ATR stop, trailed

Let's say we used two times ATR as our initial stop. We simply recalculate the stop from the latest close as the bet moves in our favour.

2. Support / resistance stop, trailed

Using the example of the FTSE100 bet, let's say a new resistance level formed at 5940. Then we would move our stop to just above 5940.

3. Moving average stop, trailed

As the moving average moves in the same favourable direction as our bet, we move the stop to a new point just beyond it.

4. Highest high / lowest low stop, trailed

If we are using the highest high for 5 days as our stop for a down bet, then as the highest high becomes lower as our bet starts winning, then we move the stop down.

5. Money stop, trailed

If we are using a money stop we recalculate it from each new close as the bet moves in our favour.

Overall result: when a bet moves in our favour we move the stop. After a while, the stop reaches a point where we can do no worse than breakeven. A little later, the stop reaches a point where we are guaranteed a profit. And so on. We can keep a bet running for a long time if it continues to work for us, trailing our stop behind it.

Postscript

After stop losses, one thing remains before we reach that first haven of Base Camp, and that it is to get a thorough understanding of order types.

10

Spread Betting Order Types

This chapter discusses the important area of spread betting order types. If you think there is only one way of entering or exiting a bet think again!

If you are fairly new to spread betting you may find this chapter a little confusing – and just when you thought you had got it all taped. Hopefully by the end of this chapter you will be comfortable with all the different order types.

I will be illustrating the various order types with the following example–

- We have one bet already open which we intend to close: an up bet on gold which is trading currently at 635.5.

- Plus we want to open an up bet on the Dow Jones Industrial Average (DJIA) currently at 11451.5.

Market order

The simplest and most obvious order type for most people is the *market order*. A market order can be used to enter or to exit a bet. With a market order we are saying that we are happy to accept whatever the market's prevailing bid or offer price is.

Let's say we are away from our PC and have to use the old fashioned technique of phoning in to our spread betting firm. We ask for a quote on gold and get 635.2/635.8; we say we are selling and therefore we sell at 635.2. We then ask for a quote on DJIA and get 11449/11454; we say we are buying and therefore we buy at 11454. We could also have carried out these tasks online, using market orders.

Limit order

We can also specify that we wish to buy or sell at a more favourable price than the current market price. This is a *limit order*. This means we have to wait until the market moves to that more favourable price before we buy or sell. The advantage of this is we get a better price if the market does indeed move that far, but the risk is that the market may never move that far and we will not get filled (i.e. we will end up without the order being executed).

Let's say we want to close our up bet on gold only if it reaches 648.0 We can place a limit order to sell at 648.0. And we want to buy DJIA at a better price than it is currently; we place a limit order to buy at 11425. Most spread betting firms offer two types of limit order–

1. *GTC*: Good Till Cancelled, if we choose this type, our two orders will sit in the firm's trading system indefinitely unless we cancel them or the limit price is reached. If gold reaches 648.00 our bet will automatically be executed and our gold bet sold, and if DJIA reaches 11425 an up bet will automatically be opened for us.

2. *Good for the day*: if we choose this type the orders will be automatically closed at the end of the day if the limit prices have not been reached.

Stop order

Alternatively we can specify that we wish to buy or sell at a less favourable price than the current market price. This is a *stop order*. People new to this game sometimes find these stop orders a little surprising.

Why would we want a worse price?

Using the stop order to exit

By now you are hopefully convinced of the merits of stop losses. We use a stop order in the spread betting firm's trading platform to set our stop loss to be triggered automatically. The stop order says "if my bet deteriorates to this point, get me out". Using our example of gold let's say that if gold goes down to 620.00 we will take that as a sign that our up bet is not working. We therefore set a stop order at 620.00.

Remember, we also just set a limit order to exit if price improves to 648.0. We can have a limit order and a stop order on the same instrument. If we do that in this example we are cashing in at 648.00 and bailing out at 620.00.

We have got gold surrounded!

The only problem is, if we are not watching the market, we might find gold goes up to 648.0 and down to 620.0; we sell at both prices and therefore end up short. [There is a solution to this problem offered by some firms, which is the OCO order, discussed later in this chapter.]

Using the stop order to enter

We can also use the stop order to enter a new bet, at a worse price than currently. Eyebrow's raised? Did we just say at a *worse* price? Surely we want a better price than now?

Let's construct a scenario using our DJIA example. Current price 11451.5. We believe a move upwards is likely. However, rather than just taking a punt and entering immediately we decide we will wait for DJIA to give us a positive sign that it's time to enter an up bet. We decide that the sign we are looking for is for DJIA to exceed the high price of the previous day, which is 11461. So we set a stop order to buy at 11462. This means that no trade is executed while the DJIA remains below 11462, but as soon as the Index hits that level, then the trade is executed as a market order – i.e. go long at the prevailing offer price in the market.

We have a trade off here – we have entered at 10.5 points worse than the current price, on the other hand we have let DJIA prove itself by setting off in the right direction for an up bet. [We will be covering this principle in depth in Part2.]

Guaranteed stop loss order

Here is a variation on a theme.

Many people new to spread betting are worried that if they put a stop into the firm's trading system there is no guarantee their bet will be closed exactly at the stop point. The market may be moving fast at the time and some slippage may occur on their stop order; or the market may gap past their stop. These concerns are understandable, since either of those things may occur; however the impact of them is very rarely as much as people fear, provided one sticks to the more liquid instruments.

But for those who want to purchase peace of mind the spread betting firms provide the guaranteed stop loss order – at a cost. The guaranteed stop loss order is put in place at the same time as a bet is entered, and the firm guarantees that the bet will be exited at no worse than the price at which the stop loss order is placed. The trade off cost for this peace of mind is however a significantly worse spread.

Back to our example. The quote for entering the DJIA guaranteed stop loss bet is 11444.5-11458.5; a 14 point spread for an index. Why pay away a 14 point spread on a highly liquid instrument like DJIA when you can get a 2 to 4 point spread on a simple rolling daily bet and put your own stop in? It would surprise me if the number of winning spread bettors who use guaranteed stop loss orders is that large.

More recent innovations in order types

Recently, more sophisticated order types have been introduced by some of the innovative firms. These include:

Contingent order

One order is only put in place when another has been triggered.

Using our DJIA example, let's say we want to enter an up bet on a stop order if the price reaches 11462. But at the same time, if our up bet is triggered we also want to put a stop loss in place at say 11360. A contingent order allows us to do that. There are effectively two orders in the trading system–

1. order one: buy on a stop at 11462;

2. order two: sell on a stop at 11360.

Order two is linked to order one and contingent on order one being filled; if order one is not triggered, order two won't be either.

OCO order (one cancels the other)

With an OCO order (once cancels the other) there are effectively two orders held in the trading system, linked to each other. If one order is triggered the other one is automatically cancelled.

This solves the problem we looked at earlier: we had a stop order to sell on our gold up bet at 620.0 (in case the bet moved adversely) but also had a limit order to sell at 648.0 (in case the bet moved favourably). An OCO order in this situation allows both orders to sit in the system simultaneously and to be linked to each other. If our stop order at 620.0 is triggered, the limit order is cancelled; if our limit order at 648.0 is triggered our stop order is cancelled.

Take profit stop

This is a cross between a contingent order and a limit order. A predetermined point may be set to exit at a profit. This point can be established after opening a bet or it can be linked in advance to a limit or stop order to open a bet.

If we applied a Take Profit stop to our gold bet at 648.0 this would work exactly as a limit order to sell placed at that point.

With the DJIA example, let's say we decide to enter on a stop order at 11462; we could also, in advance, place a Take Profit order at say 11670; the Take

Profit order would only be triggered if the stop order to enter the bet had already been entered; this is similar in concept to a contingent order.

Trailing stop

This allows a stop loss to be automatically moved as the market moves in favour of the bet.

The spread betting firm Global Trader is the only firm at the time of writing to offer this facility – the trailing stop can be initiated, edited or removed at any time while the position is open. The trailing stop facility can also be applied to Guaranteed Stop Losses.

Let's look at our up bet on DJIA. Let's say we open the bet with a market order at 11454 and decide at the same time that we want to run a trailing stop loss on it. We decide the distance from it to set the initial stop – let's say we set it 11360 (94 points away); and we decide the increments that we wish to trigger the trailing stop – let's say we choose 10. The net result will be every time the bet moves 10 points in our favour the stop will be automatically moved up 10, to stay 94 points away. When DJIA trades at 11464, our stop will be moved to 11370. When DJIA trades at 11474 our stop will be moved to 11380. And so on. Our stop will never be moved down (once it reaches 11380 for example it can only be moved up, never back to 11370).

An excellent facility and one which I hope will be introduced by other spread betting firms in due course.

Stop limit order

We don't have these yet in spread betting, but hopefully it will only be a matter of time before an innovative firm introduces them.

Normally, when a stop order is activated, it becomes a simple market order – i.e. buy (sell) at whatever the prevailing offer (bid) is in the market. But a *stop limit* order is a stop order that becomes a limit order when activated. This allows for greater control of the order. The purpose is protection from those times when the market is moving so fast that when a stop order is activated, the market price is quickly far away from the stop level price.

With the DJIA example, if we set a stop limit order to enter an up bet at 11462, then nothing will happen unless the price gets up to 11462 (just like a stop order). However once the stop point of 11462 is reached, our order is transformed into a limit order. So we will either be filled at 11462, or not at all.

Are some orders better than others?

Each type of order can be useful at different times and for different people.

Orders for opening bets

- If you feel you have to open a bet right now for whatever reason you will probably use a **market order**. You will open a position, even if not at the best price that could have been achieved.

- If you feel that you can get a better entry price than the current price, you will use a **limit order**. Such orders may be used if your trading methodology requires very precise entry and exit prices. The obvious danger is that price will never get back to the level of the limit order, and you will miss out on the trade.

- If you want price to set off in the right direction, or to break through some critical level on the chart, before you enter then you will use a **stop order**.

- If you want to set a stop loss simultaneously with entering the bet (and you are not using a market order) then you will use a **contingent order**.

- If price is currently in a range and you want to go either long or short depending on whether the instrument breaks up or down out of the range then you will use an **OCO order**.

Automated orders to enter come into their own if you don't have the time to monitor the markets intraday. The spread betting account will be on auto pilot and will enter the bet for us in our absence.

Orders for closing bets

- If you have mental stops, rather than automated stops, you will probably exit using a **market order**. Your discipline has to be good, otherwise you find you ignore the mental stops and suddenly run up an excessively large loss.

- If you have a target in mind for exiting at a more favourable price you will set a **limit order** to exit.

- If you feel you should automate the stop losses then you will set them using a **stop order**.

- If you want to have in force both a stop order (automated stop loss) and a limit order (to exit after price has improved for us) then you will use an **OCO order**.

Once again, automated orders to exit come into their own if you don't have the time to monitor the markets intraday. Great for busy people.

Summary of order types

Here is a table providing an overview of the order types we have looked at.

Table 10.1: summary of order types

Order type	Use for entries	Use for exits	Comments
Market	Enter now at prevailing market price	Exit now at prevailing market price	Many people only use this type – worth learning to use other types
Limit	Enter at a more favourable price than the prevailing market price	Exit at a more favourable price than the prevailing market price	The risk is that the more favourable price never gets reached
Stop	Enter at a worse price than the prevailing market price	Exit at a worse price than the prevailing market price	Most often used for stop loss purposes
Guaranteed stop	Enter now at prevailing price with a guaranteed stop in place	Stop entered at time of entry	Expensive route to placing a stop loss – learn how to use the "ordinary" stop facilities
Contingent	Only execute this order if another linked order is executed	Only execute this order if another linked order is executed	Most common use is to place stop loss automatically and simultaneously when a linked entry is triggered
One cancels the other (OCO)	Whichever of two linked orders is executed, then cancel the other one	Whichever of two linked orders is executed, then cancel the other one	Most common use is to place orders to exit both above and below the current price, one as a stop loss, the other to take profits
Take Profit Stop	Not used for entry order	Exit at a more favourable price	Similar in principle to a limit order
Trailing Stop	Not used for entry order	Trails an automated stop according to a predefined algorithm	Great innovation, but value depends on flexibility of algorithm
Stop Limit	When price reaches a certain level, place a limit order	When price reaches a certain level, place a limit order	Not yet available, but would be very useful

What's on offer in the market?

Pretty well all the firms offer, in addition to market orders, automated limit orders and stop orders. Contingent orders and OCO orders are relatively new developments and have provided some of the newer entrants to the market place with a chance to offer something new which adds real value. Due to the competitive nature of the market place we can expect most participants to respond in due course to the new developments by ensuring their range of available order types matches customer demand.

It is worth pointing out that the sophistication of order types in spread betting has at least temporarily outclassed that available in the UK from stock broking firms.

Postscript

This has been a complex chapter, and you will be in a minority if you have absorbed all the points in one go. Knowing the pros and cons of the different order types and when to use them is important. Many spread bettors just use market orders to enter, and don't automate their stops. They mostly don't get as far as Base Camp.

The final chapter in Part One deals with a range of practical issues to do with running a spread betting account.

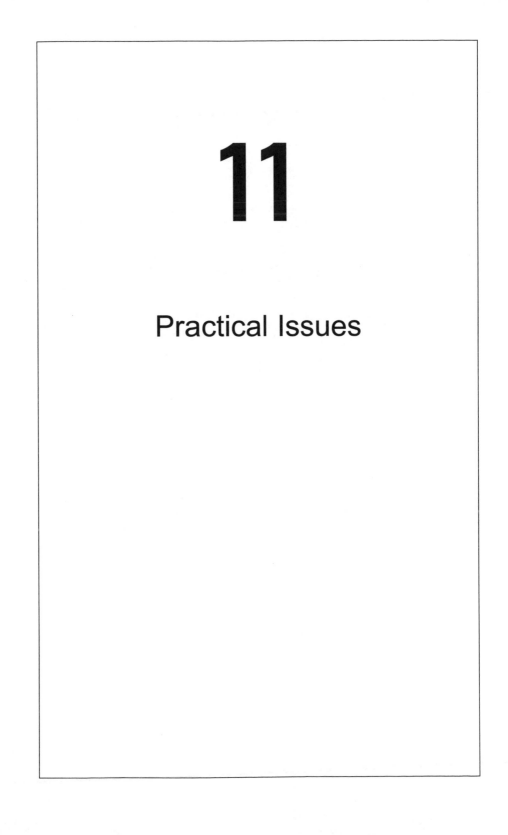

11

Practical Issues

In this chapter we deal with some practical issues in running a spread betting account, under the headings of

- order placement,

- automated stop losses,

- dispute resolution, and

- account funding.

If you are very new to spread betting you may want to skim through this chapter noting what issues are covered, read the ones which are currently relevant to you, and then return to the chapter at a later time.

Order placement

Placing orders online

Write down all the bets you are planning to make before you place them, and then also write them down as you place them. Make sure you have written down the instrument, the bet size and whether you are a buyer or a seller.

Why?

Writing them down beforehand gives you a check list to make sure you make all the bets you intend to make (and nothing else). Writing them down as you make them allows you to check them against your pre-prepared checklist and later to check they have all been processed correctly and to ensure all your records are up to date.

Your prepared checklist is particularly important if you are placing large bets and decide you want to place them across more than one firm, or place them over a period of time. You will be able to know at any point in time how much of your total planned order you have already placed. If you are placing orders across several firms make sure that you write down the firm used for each order as well as the instrument, the size and whether you are a buyer or a seller.

One click or two?

Some firms give you a choice of–

1. **"one click"**: places the order immediately you click on the button to place the order.

2. **"two click"**: adds an intermediate step; you first indicate what order you want (first click) then your order is summarised and you have to click again to confirm it (second click) – your order is only placed on the second click and if for some reason you fail to make the second click you won't have placed a bet.

I personally always use "two click" order placement if it is available – I want that intermediate step in there to check the bet is the one I intended. "One click" is obviously faster but I prefer less risky to faster in this case.

Re-quotes

A *re-quote* occurs online when you decide to buy or sell an instrument based on the price you see on the screen, and then back comes a message telling you that the price is in fact different.

Frustrating!

With some firms you don't get re-quotes. The price you see on the screen is the one you get if you take the bet. With other firms you do get re-quotes.

Let's look at the various reasons you could get a re-quote:

1. The market is moving fast and the price in the underlying market has moved against you; this happens – it's a fact of trading life.

2. The market is moving fast and the price in the underlying market has moved in your favour; this also happens – although seemingly not so often!

3. The underlying market quote, on which the spread betting quote is based, is based on relatively small size and if you were dealing in the underlying market you would not be able to get the existing quotes for all your order. In other words, you would move the market with your order; this can happen with larger orders, or when the market is very quiet. Possible solutions here are either to subdivide your order and place it at different times; or to put in limit orders to ensure you get the price you want.

4. A variation on the last point, a number of other customers are trying to make the same bet as you, so in aggregate your total order exceeds the orders sitting in the underlying market place; so in aggregate the customers' orders would move the market, and the re-quote reflects this. Same solution as for the previous point.

5. The firm has decided to add something to its spread now it knows whether you are long or short. The spread of the bet is in effect out of line with the underlying market, either skewed in the direction you are going, or just wider both ways. This is the irritating one, but as competition increases, the firms that do this regularly will find their customers starting to use other firms. You will perhaps recall that in the chapter on resources I mentioned that I have a data feed that gives me the live prices of the underlying market. As a result I am always able to compare the spread betting quote with the underlying market. If the re-quote is unacceptable to me (i.e. too far off the underlying market) I generally refuse the re-quote and try again a short while later; or put in a limit order for the price I want. I don't usually miss out on the bet because of this, but if I do it's usually no big deal. I move on.

Placing orders on the phone

Most spread bettors place their orders online these days rather than phoning them in. It is a lot easier for most people.

But there will be times when, for whatever reason, you don't have access to online facilities and you want to place bets over the phone. This should be a straightforward process. However, there a few tips which should help prevent any accidents–

1. Write down what bet you want to make before you make the call; from time to time people get themselves in a muddle on the phone and say something different from what they intended – you are less likely to do that if you are reading from your pre-prepared script. Make sure you have written down the instrument, your bet size, whether you are buying or selling and the order type.

2. Make sure you have your account details with you before you make the call; you will be wasting your time and the dealers' if you try to place a bet without those details.

3. Be aware that your call will usually be recorded.

4. Also be aware that the dealers can't give you any advice, so don't waste your time or theirs trying to get some.

5. Speak deliberately clearly and slightly more slowly than usual during the call.

6. When you get through to the dealer first of all ask him or her to quote for the instrument – clarify what size you want but don't reveal whether you are buying or selling. Keep the request for a quote short and to the point. Here is an example: "please can you quote me for October Vodafone, £100 per point".

7. You will then get a quote from the dealer, which will usually just consist of 2 numbers. If you are not sure you have heard it properly ask the dealer to repeat it, but bear in mind quotes are time sensitive so try not to waste time. You need to be fully familiar with what the two numbers you receive represent – the lower number is what you sell at and the higher number is what you buy at. An easy way to remember this is you will always be using the number which is worse for you! You need to decide quickly if you want to accept the quote or not.

8. If you decide to accept the quote then read from your script adding the price you have just received. For instance, if your Vodafone quote has come back 130-131, and you want to buy, your script will say Buy October Vodafone £100 per point, and you will say to the dealer, " Buy October Vodafone at 131, £100 per point".

9. If on the other hand you decide not to accept the quote then just say, "Nothing there".

10. If you have accepted the quote make sure the dealer reads back to you the bet you are making and check the bet against your pre-prepared script – the dealers are trained to double check your bet with you so this should happen without you prompting, but it is essential. If there is any discrepancy sort it out there and then.

11. Keep your written script until you can check the transaction has gone through to your account correctly either online or via a statement or confirmation.

12. If when you check the transaction you believe there has been an error on the part of the dealer, phone the customer service or help desk as soon as you spot it. If you do this straightaway and your bet has been incorrectly

processed they will be able to identify this by listening to the recording of your phone call.

13. If you made a mistake and phoned in a bet incorrectly, then unfortunately that's your problem not theirs – don't expect the spread betting firm to undo the bet.

14. Also if you make a bet on the phone you won't be able to change your mind after the dealer has confirmed it with you; if you realise instantly that you have made a mistake you are going to have to close the bet in the usual way and it will cost you the spread plus or minus any movement in the instrument before you close the bet.

Does this all seem a bit cumbersome? It is in fact straightforward, but you might find it is worth practising with a couple of very small bets to get comfortable with the process; and writing down the bet before you phone in does give you an extra safeguard against accidents.

Certain times of the day...

Are certain times of the day better for placing spread bets than others?

Out of hours

First of all, out of hours. You will find some firms are open 24 hours and also allow you to make bets when the market for the underlying instrument is closed. In general you will find the spreads increase in this situation, and you might be better off placing an automated order to be executed in the next period when that underlying market is open.

Market open

For smaller stocks, including many of the FTSE350 stocks, the spreads tend to be wider at the start of the day, particularly if the order book is very thin. You might well find that you can get better spreads and better prices in the afternoon. Be particularly wary of the first half hour to hour of the trading day in this regard. You will also find that if you have an automated stop on such an instrument and it is too close to the price it may get hit in the first half hour because of these wide spreads.

Lunchtime

Some markets tend to go quiet at lunchtime, and this can be a good time to place bets. An instrument may have had a good run during the morning, reaching the point at which you want to enter a bet, but drift slightly downwards during lunchtime as potential buyers who might put upward pressure on the price are occupied elsewhere. You can test this theory for the instruments in which you are interested if you have intraday data.

End of day

A lot of people use the end of the trading day to close or open bets, so for instance between 4.00p.m. and 4.30p.m. in the UK stock market can be hectic. You might occasionally find it harder or slower to get through on the phone to the spread betting dealing room at that time, although I have not noticed any deterioration in online trading.

Close of US markets

9.00p.m. This is when the US stock markets close, and I like to keep a check on what has happened irrespective of whether I have any bets open on US stocks, as there is often a knock-on effect on UK and European markets the next day.

Automated stop orders

This section is about stop orders that you enter into your spread bettor's trading platform – to be executed when you may not be watching the market. These are distinct from stops that you mentally track that prompt you to then input market or limit orders.

Compulsory stop losses

One or two firms are starting to insist that their clients automate their stop losses.

The approach at Capital Spreads and at Global Trader, for example, is to insist that a stop loss is formally in place on every trade. The upside here is that you are forced to use the stop loss discipline. The downside is that you do not have the discretion to use a mental stop.

Prices used for stop losses

Different firms use different prices to trigger a stop loss. For example, some use:

- the bid and offer prices in the underlying market;

- the actual trades in the underlying instrument; or

- their own bid and offer prices. In this case, because the firms' spreads are generally wider than the underlying market, the stop could be triggered without the bid or offer price in the underlying market ever reaching that level.

Other firms even give you a choice of how you want your stop triggered, on a stop by stop basis. The important point is to know the ground rules for the firm you are using.

> From a personal point of view I prefer my automated stops to be triggered by something in the underlying market, which I can observe independently, rather than by an internally generated spread betting firm's price.

Market maker activity

Be aware that in the underlying markets (on which bets are based) market makers are often well aware of where there is a likely to be a bunch of stops.

For example, if a stock has a well-established resistance line at 100, then it's quite likely that there could be a bunch of stop buy orders around that level (some of those could be stop losses for short positions, and the rest stops to open long positions as the stock breaks up through the 100 level). If market-makers know that there are a bunch of stops on a stock at 100p, the stock is rising and they want to acquire the stock, then they might initially force the market lower through some large sell orders, get the price down to 100p, pick up a load of stock at 100p and then let the stock continue its upward path.

For that reason it is sometimes wise not to put your stops in obvious places such as at round numbers e.g. 100p.

Spread betting firm activity

A variation on the above theme.

You might be concerned that if you have a stop with a spread betting firm it might get taken out by them even without the underlying market trading there. Over the years there has been occasional speculation that this might be a cause for concern. There are four points to mention here–

1. In today's competitive market a firm would be concerned about acquiring a reputation amongst its customers for this sort of activity.

2. In a good spread betting firm's business plan retaining customers is likely to be a priority, since acquiring new customers is expensive.

3. Spread betting is regulated by the FSA, and the firm would not want an unhappy customer complaining to them about this sort of activity.

4. Each firm should have a compliance department, which is there to sort out anything like this – have a look at the section on dispute resolution below.

Order cancellation

If you have automated stop and limit orders held for you by your spread betting firm, there is one critical point–

In general they do not get automatically cancelled if you exit a bet, even if you only put them in originally because you had a bet in place.

They are usually held as separate and distinct orders on the system. For example you may have a sell stop in place to protect you from an adverse move on an existing up bet; if you close the up bet via a market order, don't forget to also remove the sell stop; otherwise you may shortly become the proud but surprised owner of a down bet on that instrument.

Dispute resolution

Once in a while you may find you have a disagreement with a spread betting firm. This has been a very rare occurrence for me personally over the years, however it is worth knowing what to do if you do have a dispute. The procedure is–

1. The first port of call is the **customer service desk** or help desk. Don't try to bypass them, because they will be able to resolve most problems. If for some reason they can't resolve the issue, then

2. each firm should have a **compliance department**. If they can't resolve your dispute,

3. the next stop is probably the **MD**. And finally,

4. you can refer your complaint to the **Ombudsman** and the **FSA**.

My personal experience has been in three areas.

Firstly, back in the early days, when most bets were placed over the phone, I had a number of bets which were not as I thought I had made them. Every one of those issues was resolved by the helpdesks of the four firms involved, and resolved promptly and courteously. In each case, except one, a dealer had made an error and the transaction was adjusted back to what it should have been. In the other case it was a little ambiguous and they gave me the benefit of the doubt.

The second area involved an automated stop which had been triggered in the first few minutes of trading and it looked to me like the market hadn't actually traded where the stop was. The helpdesk on this occasion put me straight on to the dealer who had triggered the stop and we walked through all the trades that had actually occurred in the underlying market. I realized that although he had been a bit quick on the trigger, he hadn't done anything wrong technically and that there would be no point in complaining to the compliance department. This was a small stock with a lot of volatility and I realized that for this stock I either needed in future to keep the stop a lot further away or I needed to manage the stop on a manual basis. So I learnt something from the experience.

The third area involved a stop on the FTSE 100 where

1. the stop was at a round number, where potentially a lot of other spread bettors had placed their stops, and

2. there had been an unusual spike in the prices of the spread betting firm, apparently not mirrored in the underlying market or in any other spread betting firm's prices, but just enough to take out my stop then retreat back to the "normal" level.

The spread betting firm were fully covered by the small print in the wording of the contract. I was fortunate enough to learn two things from this experience. I learnt at first hand that it can be dangerous to put stops exactly where a lot of other people have put their stops. And I learnt I needed to switch my business to another firm.

Funds transfers

Most firms have online funds transfer facilities. To use these you will need to designate a bank account for transferring funds to and from your spread betting account. If you prefer not to use such online facilities then funds can be transferred into your spread betting account in several ways: you can send in a cheque, or most firms will be able to process a debit card transaction on the phone. Most of them will usually take credit cards, but this tends to attract a transaction charge which seems a pointless waste of money. To get your money out you can also phone in to have a cheque sent to you.

Keep abreast of your margining position

On the general topic of money in your account, it is essential to keep on top of your margin position. If you are surprised by a request to put more money into your account, you are not fully in control of your betting. You should always know what your total margin requirement figure is and how much you have got to spare in your account. Also bear in mind that there are variations between the firms in how they calculate your total requirement for margin – some will offset winning and losing trades, some will take into account any automated stops you have in place, some will take into account the mix and concentration of your positions. Know the ground rules for the firm you are using!

Postscript

This chapter has covered a fairly diverse set of issues. It was best to get them on the table up front, but equally you may find some of the points raised worth coming back to later.

Congratulations!

As we set off to climb the mountain called Spread Betting, we are approaching Base Camp. We now have knowledge of

- both the advantages and the risks of spread betting
- how not to do it, by looking at some of the most common pitfalls
- what the spread betting firms offer

- what we can bet on and the types of instruments available

- timescales for our bets

- the choice of firms with which to open an account

- we have opened at least one account

- selected the resources we need by way of hardware, software and information

- we understand the importance of stop losses for spread betting

- we have done our homework on order types.

Congratulations on getting this far. You have already got a lot further than many people.

Sadly though, Base Camp has a high drop out rate. Some people never quite get there, others get there, lose a bit of money and give up. Others still try to bypass it and find themselves lost on the mountain with no support. Often this is because they don't have any strategies for entering and exiting bets. And that's what we start looking at in Part 2.

PART 2

Climbing
The Mountain

Part 2 – Climbing The Mountain

Now we start our journey up the face of the mountain.

This is where we have to put all our equipment to use. Now we need to choose what strategies we will use to determine which bets we will place. If we are to be successful and make our way up the mountain we need our strategies to give us an edge. This is the main substance of Part 2.

12

Finding A Strategy
That Works For You

In this chapter we take a broad view of the types of strategy which are possible with spread betting. Types of strategy include trend following, counter trend and delta neutral. But first we take some time out to consider the individual's preferences, and to confirm the role of technical analysis in our thinking.

What do you like?

Before we look at any strategies take a few moments to consider your own preferences. Here are five areas to think about:

1. Length of bets

What timescale are you mostly likely to feel comfortable operating in? Are you attracted or appalled by the idea of getting in and out of a bet in the same day? Or does a month seem a long time to hold a bet? Are you likely to be with the majority of spread bettors who operate in the medium timescale (four to thirty days)?

2. Available time

How much time do you have during the day to monitor prices and take action on your spread bets? The very short timescale (intraday) and the short timescale (one to three days) require significant time input, and are therefore not very practical for someone with a busy day job.

3. Resources

How good are your hardware, software and data feeds? Forget intraday bets unless you have the appropriate resources and an account size which can afford them.

4. Discipline

How good are you likely to be at the essential risk management tasks such as setting and observing stop losses? Counter trend strategies require great discipline in getting out promptly at the appropriate time.

5. Experience

Beginning spread bettors dream of nailing turning points, catching the bottoms and tops. The reality is that trend following strategies are easier for the beginner; find a trend that has already started, then follow it. If the trend continues after a bet is placed it can compensate for sloppiness in the timing of the bet.

It is worth taking a short break at this point to reflect on these five areas. Consider where you stand on each of them, and whether you have any clear cut preferences at this early stage. As an example, many people conclude at this stage that they are going to give the intraday betting a miss for the time being.

Technical analysis is excellent for spread betting

What is technical analysis?

Here is a definition of technical analysis–

> *"Technical analysis is the study of market action, primarily through the use of charts, for the purpose of forecasting future price trends".*

Technical Analysis of the Financial Markets, John J Murphy

Why is technical analysis excellent for spread betting?

By studying recent market action we can better understand the forces of supply and demand affecting it. Are buyers or sellers stronger? And are they getting even stronger, or are they beginning to weaken? Is it the buyers or the sellers that will be dominant during the period for which we are considering opening a bet?

Why we won't be using fundamental analysis

In the long run prices are driven by fundamental factors. But long run here is usually beyond the timescales for spread betting. Valuation anomalies identified by investment analysts can take months to years to play out. The timescale for spread betting is usually hours, days or weeks. So, for instance, we won't be looking at the staple diet of the stock market fundamental analyst: earnings, growth, sales, profit margins, return on equity.

The raw data of technical analysis

Technical analysis can seem a little esoteric. But the raw data of technical analysis is straightforward. For any period of time we care to look at there are only a limited number of pieces of data that form the basis for the subsequent analysis.

For example, take a stock – let's use the example of a daily chart. For each day the raw data we use to form the chart are: the opening price, the closing price, the highest price of the day, the lowest price of the day, and the volume of shares traded. If you have charting software you will no doubt be familiar with a whole host of indicators, oscillators, trend lines, moving averages and so on, and also perhaps be familiar with a range of patterns which some analysts look for on the charts, such as head and shoulders patterns, double bottoms, triangles and so on. These are all derived from a combination of one or more types of the raw data of open, close, high, low and volume.

The two most common ways of representing this data on a chart are the bar chart and the candlestick chart.

Example of daily bar chart

Each bar represents one day's action. The top of each bar is the highest price reached on the day, the bottom is the lowest price. The horizontal lines on each bar are the opening price, on the left, and the closing price, on the right. The volume is usually shown as a histogram beneath the price bars.

Here is a chart showing 3 months of daily bars for the house builder Persimmon PLC.

Chart 12.1: example of a bar chart

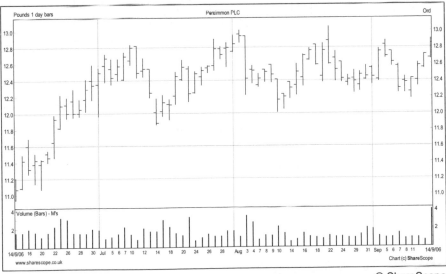

© ShareScope

Example of candlestick chart

Each candle represents one day's action. The top and bottom of each candle show the highest and lowest price achieved on the day. The wide part of each candle show the range between the closing and opening price. If the close is higher than the open, this wide part is white, if the close is lower than the open, this wide part is black. (Note, some software packages use different colours, or allow you a choice).

Here is a chart showing exactly the same 3months of daily bars for the housebuilder Persimmon PLC.

Chart 12.2: example of a candlestick chart

© ShareScope

Generally, candlestick charts are easier on the eye, and most people – once they have started using them – stick with them, preferring them to bar charts.

And a reminder: all the many and various techniques of technical analysis are derived ultimately from the fairly simple data shown in a candlestick chart. High, low, open, close and volume.

The basic choice: trend or countertrend strategies?

Once we have decided that we will be using technical analysis to inform our spread betting decisions, we still have to think through how we want to use it.

And this will depend a lot on our own personal risk profile and personality. We first have to decide whether we want to trade with or against a trend.

Trading with the trend

If we trade with a trend we have a number of key steps to take-

1. identify a trend

2. find a suitable way of entering the trend

3. identify the point at which we will deem the trend to have at least temporarily ended, and establish an appropriate exit point based on our risk management rules

4. determine bet size

5. identify an initial profit target

6. ensure the potential reward versus the potential risk is acceptable

7. ride the trend

8. move our stop loss points as appropriate

9. pyramid (add to our position) if appropriate

10. identify an appropriate exit point after riding the trend

If we trade with a trend we will be entering established trends. Some of the trend will by definition already have taken place-

- in an **up trend** we will *buy high* and *sell higher*

- in a **down trend** we will *sell low* and *buy lower*

If we trade with a trend and get our timing wrong we might get baled out of a poor entry as the trend eventually catches up.

But there is rarely just one trend for a financial instrument. Trends operate in a large number of timeframes. For example, while the trend on the weekly chart may be up, the trend on the daily chart may be down, with trends on the hourly and five minute charts neutral and up respectively.

Trading against the trend

If we trade counter to the trend we have another set of key steps to take–

1. identify key support or resistance that is likely to halt any existing trend

2. identify an appropriate entry point

3. identify the point at which support or resistance will fail and we will therefore exit

4. determine bet size

5. identify an initial profit target

6. ensure the potential reward versus the potential risk is acceptable

7. ride the counter trend movement

8. move our stop loss points as appropriate

9. pyramid (add to our position) if appropriate

10. identify an appropriate exit point after riding the counter trend movement

If we trade against a trend we will be taking positions against a dying or dead trend just before it reverses–

- trading against an **up trend** we will *sell high* and *buy low*

- trading against a **down trend** we will *buy low* and *sell high*

If we trade against a trend we have to be super quick if we are wrong since the trend will continue to erode our account balance.

As a basic principle of risk management it is usually safer to trade with the trend, and if we trade against a trend it is safer to have a longer term trend on our side. For example, if we bet on resistance stopping an up trend on the hourly chart we are safer doing this if the trend on the daily and weekly charts is down.

We will be looking at using spread betting both to ride trends and to bet on reversals of trends; we will also be looking at some intraday strategies.

Or delta neutral strategies

There are also a number of strategies available for those that prefer to eliminate trends from the equation. A delta neutral strategy is one where the success of the strategy is not dependent on the overall upward or downward movement of the market.

We will be looking at a number of delta neutral strategies, including pairs trading, arbitrage and hedging.

Master one strategy first

It might appear tempting when presented with a large range of potential spread betting strategies to have a go at all of them. This is unlikely to be successful. It takes time to become proficient at any of them. **Some of the most successful spread bettors only have one strategy, but they know it inside out and they execute it well, day in day out, repetitively.** It might even seem boring. But it is right for them. They know their risk profile, they know their area of competence and they are cashing in.

Jack of all trades and master of none.

That's the opposite of what we are aiming for here.

Postscript

In this chapter we have thought about our preferences, taking into account five key areas, we have adopted technical analysis as a tool to help us, and we have taken an overview of various spread betting strategies. We are ready to start with the first strategy: betting on a trend.

13

Spread Betting Strategy I – Betting On A Trend – Trend Identification

13

In this chapter and the next two we look at our first strategy for spread betting, betting on a trend. In this chapter we outline the concept, then look at ways of identifying trends. In the second of these three chapters we combine a number of the ways of identifying trends and illustrate how one can build a methodology to go from trend identification to bet selection. In the last of these three chapters we look at various practical issues to do with betting on a trend. This is a long and involved section of the book, covering topics which could (and indeed often has) taken whole books to cover. Don't be surprised if it takes several readings before you get to grips with it fully.

Basic concept – using spread betting to ride a trend

Here is an example of a stock in an uptrend. The stock is the mining company Kazakhmys. Note the thick black lines underneath the prices, this is where prices fell to and then turned back up. Each time we get a turning point it is at a higher level than the time before. We are looking at higher lows.

Now note the thick black lines above the prices, this is where prices rose to and then turned back down. Each time we get a turning point it is at a higher level than the time before. We are looking at higher highs.

One of the classic definitions of an uptrend is

a series of higher lows and higher highs

Please note this is only one of several different ways of defining a trend, and we shall be looking at others later in this chapter.

Figure 13.1: an uptrend, Kazakhmys

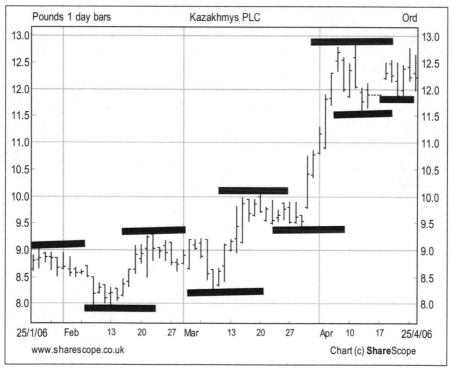

The converse is also the case. One of the classic definitions of a downtrend is a series of lower lows and lower highs. Here is an example of a stock in a downtrend. It is the food producer Northern Foods.

Figure 13.2: a downtrend, Northern Foods

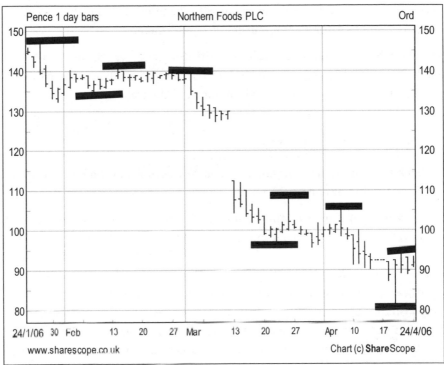

© ShareScope

In the period that these two graphs covered (which is just three months) the price of Kazakhmys increased by over 40% and the price of Northern Foods decreased by just under 40%. Even without the leverage of spread betting substantial profits were available from being long Kazakhmys and short Northern Foods during this period.

If we can identify stocks that are trending either up or down we can aim to hop on board and ride the trend. This is a very simple concept, but effective.

From a personal point of view, over three quarters of all the bets I place are attempting to do just that.

However it is not quite as straightforward as one might think at first sight. Trends always look obvious after the event, but we have to find them as they are happening, not afterwards. Also, a trend can potentially reverse at any time, so we must be fully prepared for this risk. If we hold on stubbornly after a trend has reversed we can damage our account very quickly. And again, some trends stop without reversing, the price just goes nowhere. If we are on board hoping to ride the trend and the trend peters out with the price going nowhere we want to get out and look for more promising bets elsewhere.

So even when we have successfully identified a trend, we still need to find a good place to enter; and use appropriate risk management so we keep losses small if the bet goes wrong and exit promptly if the trend stops.

Break outs or pullbacks?

Go back to those charts of Kazakhmys and Northern Foods, and look again at the thick blacks lines one more time.

One way of getting on board the trend might be to wait for the trend to confirm its power by breaking through one of those black lines – the ones above the prices in the case of the uptrend (Kazakymys), where the trend breaks through resistance, or the ones below the prices in the case of the downtrend (Northern Foods), where the trend breaks through support. If the trend is powerful enough to smash resistance or support like, that it is showing that the balance of probability is for that trend to continue. That's a simplified view of a breakout. But there is a problem with break outs – you get quite a few false break outs, where after breaking resistance or support, the trend reverses back instead of continuing.

An alternative is to enter on a pullback. In an uptrend, we wait for prices to go down a bit, and then hop on board the trend as they start to go back up again. In a downtrend, we wait for prices to rise a bit, and then hop on board the trend as they start to go back down again.

Whether you prefer to enter on break outs or pullbacks depends a lot on your personality and betting style. In this book our primary style will be to enter on pullbacks, and we will have an advantage that we will be able to clearly define the point at which our bet is not working, and thus control our risk.

How to identify trends

We have looked at a classic definition of a trend – higher highs and higher lows for an uptrend and lower highs and lower lows for a downtrend. And using that definition we could trawl through all the financial markets we are interested in to find possible candidates for a bet. Powerful trends tend to be very obvious on the screen. A quick visual inspection of a chart of each instrument might give us, in a very straightforward way, a useful shortlist of trending financial instruments.

For instance, no one looking at this chart of Tate PLC could be in much doubt that the trend for the previous 6 months had been powerfully up.

Figure 13.3: an obvious uptrend, Tate

© ShareScope

However there is a wide range of technical analysis tools which can also assist in the task of identifying trends, and you will find that many spread bettors will have their own favourites – tools which have worked for them in the past and with which they have become fully familiar. I will mention some of them below, however, first, some caveats..

Some caveats regarding technical analysis

Any technical analysis tool is only that – a tool to assist decision making, not an infallible guaranteed producer of riches. If you are hoping there is one special tool out there that will automatically produce spread betting profits, then you are going to be disappointed.

The sheer number of possible tools and techniques is quite daunting. But don't feel you have to learn them all, just find a few that you are comfortable using. There is a diminishing return as you add more and more technical analysis tools and techniques to your arsenal. For instance if you are currently using ten or more indicators to help your betting decisions that is probably too many. Some of them will probably overlap and others will give you confusing and conflicting signals.

After those important caveats, what follows is a selection of the many technical analysis tools people use to help them identify trends. This is far from a comprehensive list. The purpose of it is to show you that there are alternatives, and to encourage you to experiment a little if this is all fairly new to you. Later in this chapter I will show you a number of techniques that have worked for me. And towards the end of this book I will mention a number of books which I have found particularly valuable in developing my understanding of what is right for me and what isn't.

In the end it is up to each spread bettor to select techniques to include in their betting methodology that suit their betting style and beliefs about the markets, and what is right for me may not be right for you. You are going to have to make your own choice.

Moving averages

There are many techniques involving moving averages. For example, we can define an uptrend as–

- price being above a particular moving average; or

- we can add a further requirement that the moving average must also be sloping upwards; or

- we can use two moving averages and define an uptrend as the shorter moving average being above the longer moving average (for instance the 50 day moving average being higher than the 200 day moving average); or

- we can use three moving averages and define an uptrend as the moving averages configured with the shortest above the middle average, and the middle average above the longest average. For instance we can define an instrument as being in an uptrend when its 20 day moving average is higher than its 50 day moving average and the 50 day moving average is higher than the 200 day average.

Once we have defined our uptrend, entries can be triggered by various techniques. For instance, we can enter a new bet when –

- price moves above a moving average; or

- price pulls back to a moving average; or

- a shorter moving average crosses upwards over a longer term average.

If we are examining a downtrend then the techniques are the exact opposite. For example, we can define a downtrend as price being below a particular moving average, or we can add a further requirement that the moving average must also be sloping downwards. And so on.

This may sound quite complicated, but in practice it isn't, and moving averages have been used for a long time both by spread bettors and other traders.

Moving average aficionados tend to uniquely analyse each financial instrument they are looking at – so each instrument might have its own optimised moving average parameters. But over the years a few standards have emerged–

- for the longer term stock market investor a 50 and 200 moving average combination is popular;

- for shorter term traders a 5 and 20 day combination, also a triple combination of 4, 9 and 19 days.

But the people who use moving averages most successfully tend to do their own research into which moving averages or combinations of moving averages work best for the instruments they are trading.

Here is that graph of Kazakhmys once more, with a fifty day moving average added – notice that the moving average points up and that price stays above it except for one day; the pullbacks to the moving average would in this case have been good opportunities to enter an up bet on this stock.

Figure 13.4: moving average, Kazakhmys

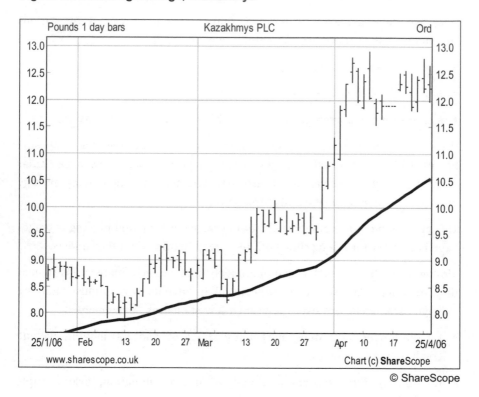

Oscillators

There is a group of indicators (called *oscillators*) which are useful for identifying relatively high or relatively low prices (overbought/oversold situations) when there is no marked trend. However some of this group can also be used to define a trend; for example, the very simple *Rate of change* indicator (which just compares today's closing price with the price x days ago, expressed as a percentage). If the Rate of change indicator is above 100, this means that today's price is higher than the price X days ago and we assume we are in an uptrend, if it's below 100 we assume we are in a downtrend. Entries can be triggered by the indicator crossing the mid (100) line. This approach tends to lead to many failed trades when the trend is not clear, as the indicator crosses back and forth across its mid line. Using another approach, assuming we have identified an uptrend, we wait for the indicator to pull back to the midline and then use this as an opportunity to get on board.

Here is an example of this second approach. Note that in this example the software labels the Rate of change indicator as "Momentum". 10 days is used in this example as a (fairly common) setting (i.e. we are comparing prices with those 10 days earlier).

Figure 13.5: Rate of change, Tate

© ShareScope

The example shows part of the powerful uptrend in Tate PLC which we looked at earlier. In the early part of the graph we are defining the instrument to be in an uptrend because the Rate of change indicator is above 100. The two arrows show two good points to have entered an up bet in Tate, where the indicator pulled back to around 100. The trend slowed down at these two points allowing more passengers to get on board but the indicator never went below 100. The later point marked by an ellipse is different because the indicator fell below 100, casting at least temporary doubt on the continuing strength of the trend.

12-month high or low

We can make an assumption that if a financial instrument makes a new high or new low for the last twelve months it must certainly at some point have been trending up or down, and it is useful to keep a list of which instruments have achieved this.

Here are two examples–

Figure 13.6: 18-month high, British Airways

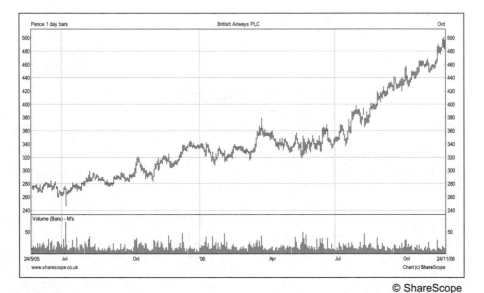

© ShareScope

An 18 month chart of British Airways, which has recently made a new high for the last 12 months, and indeed has continually been making new highs over the last few months. Visually it is obvious it has been in a powerful uptrend.

Figure 13.7: 12-month low, Plasmon

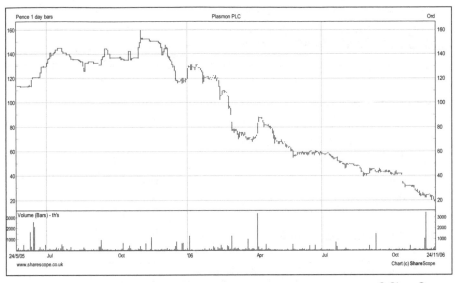

© ShareScope

A chart of Plasmon PLC, making new lows which, equally obviously, has been in a downtrend.

ADX

There are a number of indicators specifically designed to identify trends. One of the oldest of these, the ADX seems to be more widely used in the US than in Europe for some reason. The ADX is an indicator that attempts to measure the strength of a trend. [An overview of how it is constructed is included in the Appendix.]

There are two possible approaches to using this indicator for identifying trends.

1. We look at the level of the ADX indicator – the higher the level then the stronger the trend. For example, some users treat an ADX level of 30 as the cut off – above that shows the instrument is trending. But there is one more bit of the jigsaw: two linked indicators must also be in the right position, DI+ must be above DI- for an uptrend, vice versa for a downtrend.

2. We require the ADX indicator to be rising; usually with a minimum level as well, say 20. So, the ADX indicator must be above 20 and rising. (When the ADX indicator starts to fall this can be a sign that a trend is losing momentum, and prices may consolidate or even reverse).

From my own experience I have been happy just to use the level of the ADX as a trend identifier during clear bull or clear bear markets; when the broad market direction has been less clear I have added the requirement for the ADX to be rising.

If we use the ADX indicator as a trend identifier, it is important to remember that it is not infallible. It won't identify all trending instruments, and it is sometimes sluggish in indicating that a trend is over, but it does a fair job as a filter. Most of the instruments it identifies as trending will be trending, and the ones it misses we may pick up with other techniques (or they can be safely ignored).

Figure 13.8: ADX, Man Group

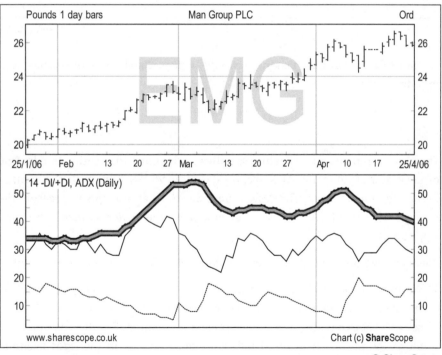

© ShareScope

Here is a chart of Man Group, with a 14 day ADX indicator added. The very thick line is the ADX, the thin line DI+, and the dotted line DI-. Note that Man Group was in a powerful uptrend during this period, and that the ADX level was above 30 throughout.

Trend lines

You will recall one definition of an uptrend was a series of higher highs and higher lows, with a downtrend being a series of lower highs and lower lows. Some analysts like to join the dots, as it were, and draw trend lines. Traditionally, analysts connect the–

1. *higher lows in an uptrend*; the uptrend is deemed to be in place as long as prices stay above the trend line.

2. *lower highs in a downtrend*; the downtrend is deemed to be in place as long as prices stay below the trend line.

Near the trendline is deemed to be a good place to enter a bet.

The art of drawing trend lines is to determine which higher lows or lower highs to connect.

Give a chart to ten analysts and you could easily get ten different trend lines!

Figure 13.9: trend line, Sainsbury

© ShareScope

Here is an example of a trend line in action. In this chart of Sainsbury we can see an uptrend in place, and a trend line has been drawn under the higher lows which occurred during this uptrend. Note that price action seems to bounce off the trend line every time there is a pull back, and during this period, pull backs to the trend line were good places to get on board with an up bet. These pull backs are marked with arrows.

Point and figure charts

Point and figure charts have a small but dedicated fan club – but given how powerful these charts are the fan club should be much bigger. [I will refer you to one of the best books on this charting technique later.]

Point and figure charts are particularly good at identifying consolidation areas and break outs from consolidation areas, either the start of a new trend or the continuation of a trend that has taken a rest.

Figure 13.10: point and figure, Kazakhmys

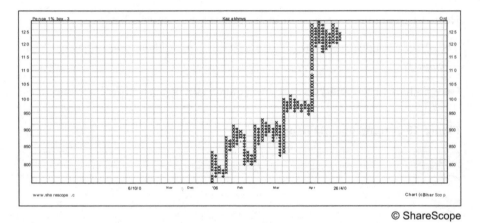

© ShareScope

Here is a point and figure chart of Kazakhmys, which covers a period similar to the one we looked at before. Note the long rising column of Xs as the stock breaks out of a consolidation area and produces the dramatic rise in price we saw before. Also note that at the far right of the chart the stock is consolidating again.

Relative strength

Relative strength (not to be confused with the Welles Wilder indicator RSI) is simply how an instrument has been performing relative to another. If, for example, a stock has been outperforming the FTSE 100 Index by 15% or more over the last three months, while it is not guaranteed that it has been in trend mode (it may have been static while the FTSE has declined) it is a pointer towards a possible trend and at the very least we would want this stock to be on our radar. Similarly, if a stock has underperformed the FTSE by 15% or more over the last three months, we will want to have it on our radar for a possible down bet.

Here are a couple of graphs, one showing an outperformer, the other showing an underperformer.

Figure 13.11: relative strength, International Power

© ShareScope

Figure 13.12: relative strength, British Energy

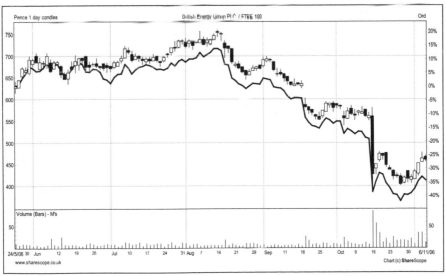

© ShareScope

Relative performance versus the FTSE100 is shown on the charts by a thick black line. The scale for the relative performance is given on the right axis. Notice how in both cases the relative performance of the stock coincided with a trend.

Visual inspection

Visual inspection of a chart – it is easy to dismiss this one if you are hooked on indicators, but some of the best trends just jump off the screen or page at you. If prices are obviously much higher on the right of your screen than on the left, and have been progressing roughly in a straight line, odds are you have spotted an uptrend; and you can apply the same logic for a downtrend if they are obviously lower. Have another look at the Tate graph again (p.139).

Don't forget: a good rule of trading is KISS - *Keep it Simple Stupid.* It's very easy to get carried away – particularly with technical analysis – and devise an over-complex trading system.

Postscript

In this first of three chapters on betting on trends we have explored the basic concept and looked at various techniques for identifying trends. In the next chapter we will put some of these together and look at a methodology to go from trend identification to trade selection.

14

Spread Betting Strategy I – Betting On A Trend – Selecting A Bet

In the last chapter we looked at various techniques for identifying trends. In this chapter we are first going to combine some of them. Then, more importantly, we are going to put together a logical way to go from trend identification to trade selection. The point of this chapter is not to provide anyone with an easy route to riches. In fact, if you are looking for that you are reading the wrong book! The point of this chapter is to illustrate how one can construct a methodology for trade selection.

In this chapter you will examine one methodology out of many possibilities. Every successful spread bettor has a methodology for trade selection. But they have all developed their own, over time. The ultimate point of this chapter is to provide some pointers to any spread bettors who either haven't yet got a methodology or haven't got one they are happy with.

Developing your own methodology for trade selection may sound like a lot of hard work. And in many ways it is. It requires research, experimentation and hard graft. It is a fact of life that to win at spread betting requires confidence: confidence in yourself, and also confidence in the system you are using.

It is an interesting psychological point that one can only have the requisite confidence if the system has been fully internalised and tailored to the individual. It has to be your system and it has to fit *your* personality and risk profile.

But I hear some voices of dissent here.

Why can't we just copy someone else's system which has been proven to work?

At some stage, if you haven't already, you will come across people offering to sell that sort of thing to you. It might seem like a good short cut. Unfortunately, most of these short cuts lead to dead ends. Usually, if the short cut seems too good to be true, it is.

One highly successful US trader is said to have taught his system to a group of up and coming traders. After a few months he checked to see how many of them were following it. Not one! Every single one had taken the basic system and adapted and modified it.

Combining techniques

As we saw in the previous chapter there are a wide range of techniques for trend identification. Here is one possible combination of techniques. It is just one combination out of many. It is one that has worked for me personally, but it is not provided as a foolproof way of making money. If anyone offers you that, be on your guard. It is provided in the context of illustrating some of the thought processes that go into developing a successful methodology for making money out of betting on trends.

Our combination of techniques for this chapter will be the following: a potential candidate for a trend-following trade will be defined as any instrument which fulfils one of the following three criteria–

1. daily **ADX indicator** being 30 or above (using a 14 day setting);

2. making new **12 month high or 12 month** low; or

3. **outperforming or underperforming** the FTSE **100** over the previous 3 months by 15% or more.

It is of course possible that some instruments will fall into two of these categories, or indeed all three.

Simplifying trade selection – the weekly shortlist

What is a weekly shortlist? It is a list we prepare on a weekly basis that includes all the instruments which fulfil the selection criteria we have adopted.

Why have a weekly shortlist?

There are two related purposes to preparing and working off a weekly shortlist. Firstly, we are attempting to ensure that all the instruments which we want to keep on our radar are there; and secondly, we are throwing everything else out, so we don't get sidetracked or waste our time on anything else. The weekly shortlist enables us to focus our time and effort on areas which according to our betting methodology give us the best chance of success.

From the above we would compile each week a shortlist comprising the three elements we discussed.

1. ADX

Over the weekend we go through the instruments we follow and pick out all those with an:

- ADX reading 30 and above, and DI+ greater than DI- (**long candidates** for the next week), and

- ADX reading 30 and above, and DI- greater than DI+ (**short candidates** for the next week).

We can do this in one of two ways: visual inspection of a chart, then adding the relevant instrument to a list (ideally using a portfolio function on our investment management software); or using computerised search facilities.

The visual inspection approach is better for many people since it has a valuable by-product: by looking at many charts we gain a better gut feel for the current state of the markets. And it is not time consuming – for example, whizzing through all 350 of the FTSE350 stocks to pick out the ones with the appropriate ADX readings should take little more than half an hour with the right sort of software.

2. 12-month highs and lows

We identify all those instruments making new highs and new lows for the last twelve months during the week. We keep these on our radar for a month. We have one portfolio of new highs and another of new lows.

3. Relative strength and weakness

To identify instruments that are outperforming or underperforming the FTSE100 by 15% or more over the last three months there are the same two methods mentioned regarding ADX – visual inspection of a chart containing a plot of relative strength (it is essential here that the relative strength over the period is quantified on the chart); or the employment of a computerised search facility. Once again, and for the same reason, visual inspection is preferred. Again this is a very quick weekly routine.

The shortlist

Let's emphasize what we are going to do with these shortlists: we are going to use them to identify potential trades. And the amount of time we are going to spend on instruments that are not on our shortlists is how much? That's right, zero.

How big are these lists going to be?

Well, they vary in size depending on what the markets are doing. As an example, at the time of writing, out of the FTSE350 stocks, about

- 70 had ADX readings over 30,

- 70 had made new highs or lows in the last month (but there was an overlap of 50 between them and the ADX list), and

- 50 were either under or over performing by 15% versus the FTSE100 (again, with a large number of these appearing on one of the other two types of list).

So, between these three types of list we have picked up all the stocks we have potential interest in and, just as importantly, we have filtered out the rest. Instead of having to trawl though 350 stocks we have narrowed our search down to less than 100. When this particular market goes quiet, sometimes the number of stocks on our three types of list can go down to in total as little as 30 out of 350.

Note: these listing techniques can be applied to whichever markets you follow: US stocks, Japanese stocks, indices, commodities, whatever.

Simplifying trade selection – identifying daily set ups

So, we now have a list of potential candidates for a bet, our weekly short list.

Our next step is every day to identify from this list any instruments that display characteristics which indicate we may want to place a bet imminently. This is commonly referred to as a "set up". Set ups only come from our short list, but only a few candidates from our short list are in set up mode at any point in time. We define specific parameters for identifying set up conditions based on our betting methodology. We will shortly give an example of a set up, and the predefined conditions which lead to it. But first, let's double check what we are doing at this stage.

From the instruments in our weekly shortlist we are now, on a daily basis, limiting the ones we are going to follow for the day to a much shorter list. We are looking for specific predefined parameters based on our betting methodology. We believe that, over time, limiting our bets to just those instruments which display those parameters will give us an edge.

Once we have identified instruments conforming to our specific predefined parameters, what do we do with all the other instruments on our weekly short list? Yes, right again, we completely ignore them for the day! We are streamlining our workload and providing focus and direction to our betting efforts.

Filtering the list down to a manageable few

Using the FTSE350 as an example, from a starting point of 350 stocks we have already reduced the number we have potential interest in for the week to let's say 100; but the number we track on a daily basis will be much less than that. Typically it might be about ten, once in a while it might be as many as twenty, and sometimes it might be just one or two. Or even zero (not very frequently, but it does happen). And if it's zero, no problem. We take the day off so far as trading is concerned. We don't try to make bets just for the sake of it, we restrict ourselves to situations where, according to our methodology, we believe we have an edge.

So what set ups do we use?

Once again, there are many possibilities out there. Technical analysis has generated a huge number of techniques for trade selection, countless indicators, moving averages, mathematical formulae employing concepts such as the Fibonacci series of numbers, plus more exotic stuff including Elliot wave, Gann squares and angles, and even astrology. It is easy to get overwhelmed by the range of choices. The good news is you only need to find one that works for you, and set ups using complicated methodology are not necessarily any more effective than the really simple ones.

One critical point at this juncture.

We are at this stage identifying set ups. There is no guarantee that any of these set ups will actually result in a trade. A set up is only a potential trade. Once we have identified our set ups we need something to happen to cause us to make a trade – a trigger. We will examine triggers shortly.

Example set up

In this chapter we will select one of the simplest possible set ups. From our weekly shortlist of instruments we will identify all those in an uptrend which have pulled back for between three and seven days from a two month high; or all those in a downtrend which have risen for between three and seven days from a two month low.

What are we doing here?

We are identifying instruments which we have defined as being in an uptrend or a downtrend and which have now had a minor correction in the opposite direction. We are using this minor correction as a potential opportunity to get on board the trend.

Why these parameters?

The logic for these parameters is as follows–

1. For an instrument to be on our weekly shortlist it already has to have some of the hallmarks of a **trending instrument**, such as a high ADX reading, or over/under performance versus a benchmark such as the FTSE 100.

2. Including a **recent two month high or low** in the parameters increases the probability that we are dealing with a trend still in force.

3. We are looking for a **real correction** rather than just random noise in the market, so we put in a minimum time for the correction to take place – in this case we have selected three days.

4. We are looking for **minor corrections** rather than major stops in the trend, so we put in a maximum time for the correction to take place – in this case we assume that if the correction lasts more than seven trading days something more substantial than a minor correction is taking place, and we no longer want to be involved.

> These parameters are ones which have worked in the past for me; however you may decide that they are not for you, and that other parameters will work better.

Example: BP

Here is an example of a set up using the above methodology.

Figure 14.1: example set up, BP

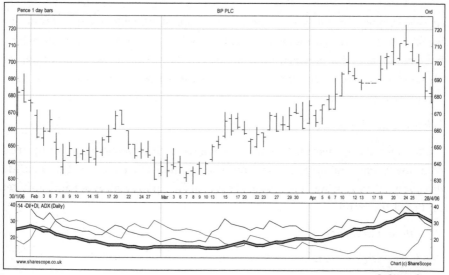

© ShareScope

BP at this point has been on our weekly short list of stocks in an uptrend with an ADX reading over 30 and DI+ greater than DI-. It has recently made a two month high. It has had a minor correction within our parameters, it has been pulling back for four days. It is at this stage only a potential bet – *we still need a trigger to take the bet.*

Taking the trade – entry triggers

Our set ups are only potential bets. For them to go from being potential bets to being actual bets, we are looking for an *entry trigger.* In this type of bet our entry trigger needs to be a sign that the correction is over and that the original trend has started again.

Once again, there are many possibilities for determining what we want our entry triggers to be, and once again we will use a simple but logical one.

In an uptrend, our entry trigger to convert a set up into an actual bet will be if the price of the instrument *exceeds* the highest price of the previous day. In a downtrend, our entry trigger to convert a set up into an actual bet will be if the price of the instrument goes *below* the lowest price of the previous day.

Once the trigger point has been reached there are several possibilities for the timing of the actual bet–

1. We can set up in advance an **automated entry** on our spread betting trading platform (since we already know the exact point of our trigger the night before). This is ideal if, for instance, we have a busy day job and won't be able to watch the markets during the day; we will find out whether we made any bets later.

2. We can place our bet **manually** either via the trading platform or via the phone as soon as we become aware the trigger point has been reached.

3. We can attempt to **fine tune** the entry if we have intraday data and the time to look at it, finding slightly more favourable entry points once the trigger point has been reached. If we try to be too clever though we may find that the trend suddenly reasserts itself strongly and whizzes past the trigger point at a rate of knots, and we end up missing out on the bet.

Let's return to the example of BP, which has pulled back for 4 days from a two month high.

The highest price on this fourth day has been 686p, that will be our trigger point, and we will place an up bet on this stock tomorrow if the price gets up to 686.25p. We will make an assumption that if price descends after our bet has been triggered to below the lowest point of the pullback, then we have made a mistake, the pullback is not yet over, and we will jettison the bet. So if we place a stop just under the lowest point of the correction (which is 676.5p), let's say at 673, our stop will be 13.25p away. We will set our initial target for the bet at the highest point of the move before the pullback. That highest point of the move before the pullback is 723p, which is 36.75p above our trigger point.

Potential 36.75p reward if the stock gets to its recent high again, while risking 13.25p – a ratio of 2.8 to 1. That's fine – a common benchmark is that this ratio should be at least 2 to 1.

Postscript

In this chapter we have built a methodology for moving from trend identification to actually betting on a trend.

We have selected a way of identifying trends; we have chosen a way to shortlist trending instruments on a weekly basis; we have selected a way of identifying set ups from that shortlist on a daily basis; and we have chosen how we will identify trigger points, stop loss points and initial targets, noting that we want at least a 2:1 ratio of potential reward to risk.

We haven't however quite made the bet yet, since there is one critical ingredient still missing.

How much are we going to bet?

15

Spread Betting Strategy I – Betting On A Trend – Bet Size

We concluded the last chapter having reached the point where we had identified a bet we wanted to make. This chapter deals with the critical issue of how much to bet. It is a short chapter, however it is one of the most important in this book. Miss your footing on this part, and you are in for a serious fall.

Taking the trade – the right size of spread bet

We have now reached the point where one of our set ups has reached its trigger point. We have made the decision that we are going to place the bet.

How much should we bet?

Here are the steps to work this out:

Step 1

Determine the price at which you will come to the conclusion that you are wrong – when you will consider the odds of the correction continuing are greater than the original trend getting going again, at least in the near future. In other words, decide where you will put your initial stop loss.

Note: in the case of BP you have already decided that a logical place to put a stop loss would be at a point a little bit beyond the furthest point of the pullback. If the price goes past the furthest point of the pullback you will assume the pullback is now not yet over, and who knows how far that pullback will continue – so you get out to preserve our capital for other more promising bets.

Step 2

Work out (in the appropriate unit) the distance from your trigger point to your stop loss point.

The appropriate unit is whatever your spread betting firm treats as being worth £1 when you bet (i.e. UK shares are £1 per penny, currencies are £1 per pip). It is of course essential that you know how this is calculated by your spread betting firm for any instrument on which you bet.

Step 3

Determine the maximum percentage of your spread betting funds that you are prepared to risk on any one bet. A commonly used rule of thumb is that this should not exceed 2%.

> Personally, I am not comfortable with this level of risk and I tend to risk about 1% only per bet.

The easiest way to understand why these figures are so low (and many people are amazed they are so low) is to consider the downside.

Extreme example case: you risk 50% per bet of your starting capital. Obviously, get two wrong in a row and you are wiped out.

Less extreme case (but still very dangerous): you risk 15% per bet of your starting capital. Even if you get 50% of your bets right you can still get a run of 5 losses in a row; indeed if you bet often it is almost certain that you will at some point. So, after 5 losses in a row, risking 15% per bet you will have under 50% of your spread betting funds left, and now you have to *double* your money just to get back to where you started. Not clever.

If you are risking just 1% of your starting capital per bet, even after 10 losses in a row you are only down about 10%, and can recover. In the first one to two years of spread betting, when a high percentage of people fail to break even, and when the broad objective is to learn to play the game well while preserving funds, it makes sense to risk less than 1% on each bet.

Step 4

Work out the actual amount in pounds that you will risk on each bet based on the percentage figure you have determined above.

Step 5

Divide the amount you are risking (as per step 4) by the distance between your trigger and your stop (as per step 2) – that is how much you should bet in pounds per point on the instrument.

Step 6

As a cross check, multiply the pounds per point (per step 5) by the current price of the instrument, that shows how much the bet is equivalent to if you were buying or selling the underlying instrument. If it turns out to be more than your account size, you have probably made an error in your calculations.

That may sound complicated, but it becomes routine. Like driving a car, a lot of things that initially seem tricky become easy to get right with a little practice, and getting your bet size right is essential to survival in the spread betting environment.

Here is a worked example which should clarify things. You will use the BP example you looked at above.

Example: calculating bet size

Step 1

You have decided that if the price drops to 673p, the correction will probably be continuing further and you will want to exit.

Step 2

UK shares are quoted by spread betting firms in pounds per point – a point is a penny for UK shares; the distance between your trigger point and your stop loss point is 13.25p (686.25 – 673); you will have 13.25 points risk.

Step 3

Let's assume you have £5000 in your spread betting account and have decided you will risk 1.25% on each bet.

Step 4

1.25% of £5000 is £62.50 – that is what you are prepared to lose on a bet on BP if you are wrong.

Step 5

Divide the total amount you are prepared to risk on this bet (from step 4) by the points risk (from step 2) and this tells us how much you can afford to bet on BP: £62.50 total permissible risk divided by 13.25 points risk is 4.7, so you would want to place an up bet of £4 per point (£5 per point if you want to be daring and round up 4.7 to 5)

Step 6

As a cross check, £4 per point times the entry trigger price of 686.25p – you have exposure to the equivalent of £2,745 worth of BP stock, less than your account size, so no obvious error in your calculations.

Summary

For those that like simple formulae, here is a summary of what we are doing–

Let R = your Risk Capital

Let P = PerCent of Risk Capital you have decided to risk on each bet

Let E = your entry price

Let S = your stop price

The amount to bet per point is–

for **longs**: (R x P/100) / (E – S)

for **shorts**: (R x P/100) / (S – E)

Substituting the figures from our example above, we get–

(5000 x 1.25/100) / 686.25 – 673   = 62.5 / 13.25

= 4.7

The question of whether to stage the entry

There is one other point to raise on the subject of bet size.

Once you have decided on the appropriate bet size, do you enter the whole bet in one go?

Or do you start with a smaller amount and then pyramid (add to your position) as the bet moves in your favour, gradually bringing the total bet up to your predetermined level? Many successful spread bettors operating in the time frames we have been discussing are happy to decide on their bet size up front and then enter it all in one go. This is certainly the simplest approach and removes the complications of dividing the bet up into parts. If the bet is split into parts you have to decide on your rules for entering each part. What percentage is each part going to be, and what are the rules for deciding how to enter each part? For many people this is one level of complexity too far – so they decide on their appropriate bet size and place the bet in one go.

Postscript

This has been a short chapter, but one of the most important. Now, finally, you have identified a bet you want to make, and have determined the right bet size. You place the bet. You are in! You have an open bet.

Now what?

The next chapter looks at how you decide when to get out of the bet.

16

When To Exit A Bet

At the end of the last chapter we finally placed a bet. This chapter looks at when to get out.

There are four scenarios to consider:

1. the bet goes against us;

2. the bet goes nowhere;

3. the reason for the bet disappears; or

4. the bet goes our way.

Just before you read this chapter, you might want to check you are completely comfortable with stop losses [explained in Part One], and the related material on order types.

1. The bet goes against us

We decided what to do here before we entered our bet. We decided on our stop loss point in advance. If price reaches our stop loss point, we get out. Either we have set an automated stop loss or, if not, when price reaches the stop loss point we place an order to exit online or phone the spread betting firm to place it.

That's what winning spread bettors do.

Losing spread bettors, on the other hand, often decide not to exit at this point, and just move the stop loss further away. This is one of the hallmarks of the losers.

2. The bet goes nowhere

This is where a time stop can be useful.

Our spread bets need to perform favourably for us within a reasonable time scale. They are not long term investments, friends or

> I exit any bet which hasn't got going after 10 trading days.

pets. If they don't work, chuck them out. Decide how long you are going to give them to perform, then if they don't, fire them!

3. The reason for the bet disappears

When we place a bet it should be for a reason, and the reason will be in line with our betting methodology. If the reason disappears and the trade is no longer valid per our methodology, it's time to reconsider. For example, if we have bet on an instrument because it has been on our weekly shortlist of instruments with an ADX reading over 30 and then conformed to our set up and entry parameters, we would want to reconsider if the ADX reading fell back below 30.

"Reconsider" – *what does that mean?*

It means looking at the recent price action and determining an exit strategy. If the instrument has been milling around going nowhere we probably want to scrub it immediately. If it has been oscillating within a range we may want to set a limit order to exit near the favourable end of the range. If it looks like it may be starting a trend in the wrong direction, then let's get out urgently. If it looks like it still has a little further to go in the right direction then we will probably want to move our stop loss in close behind it, so we try to get what is left of the favourable move but are able to exit promptly on the first sign of trouble.

4. The bet goes our way

Trade offs

Once we have placed our bet with a stop loss in place we hopefully have the downside covered. But what about the upside?

How do we decide when to take profits?

Here, as often with spread betting, there are trade offs. If we take our profits quickly we bag a winner, but we rob ourselves of any further upside. If we keep our bet on for longer we run the risk that the profit will disappear, or even worse turn into a loss. The differences between winning and losing traders are very marked

- **Losers** tend to bag a profit at the first opportunity for fear of it disappearing; meanwhile hanging on to their losing bets desperately hoping they will come good.

- **Winners** tend to get rid of the losing bets promptly, meanwhile hanging on to their winning bets and riding them for as long as possible.

Exiting at targets

One solution is to exit at predetermined targets.

While this doesn't let us ride a winner all the way, at least it enables us to bag a profit that is large enough to compensate for the risk we have taken. We can, before we make the bet, decide how many points we are risking, how many points we will get if we win and, critically, ensure that the relationship between the two is appropriate.

What is appropriate?

A fairly standard figure that is used is 2 to 1 minimum (reward to risk); but many traders prefer to use 3:1, partly to allow for slippage and partly to filter out borderline bets.

The difficulty with this approach is that we are limiting our upside on the bet. Once in a while we could potentially get a winner that doesn't just produce a reward of 3 times our risk, but runs and runs until it produces a reward of 20 times our risk. Why rob ourselves of the opportunity to get one of those really big winners? Exiting at targets comes into its own if a market is oscillating between a couple of points without trending up or down. But if we are betting on a trend we want to give ourselves the potential upside of a massive win. While still protecting ourselves from losing too much of the profit we have already got to date.

The solution is simple and elegant. We move our stop loss point as the bet moves in our favour. We employ a trailing stop loss.

The trailing stop loss

We met the trailing stop loss in Part One. A trailing stop loss is a stop loss that we move nearer to current prices as the bet goes in our favour. It is a superb tool for maximising our upside while continually controlling our downside.

Many of the issues we looked at regarding stop losses in Part One apply also to the trailing stop loss–

- Do we hard code it or have it as a mental stop?

- How close should it be?

- On what price do we base it?

- Is it an instant stop or delayed?

Whatever we decided were the answers to these questions can be applied also to the trailing stop. But there is also a lot of flexibility with the trailing stop loss.

We can base it on a different approach to our initial stop loss. For instance, we might use a support and resistance stop for the initial stop loss, but then use a money stop for the trailing stop loss. We might say, for example,

- Once in profit we will trail a stop so that the difference between the latest close and the latest trailed stop is always 1% of our betting funds. Or,

- Trail a stop so that 50% of the maximum profit achieved on the bet to date is preserved if the stop gets hit. Or,

- Trail a stop a certain percentage away from the most favourable point the bet has reached since we entered it.

We can vary the distance of the trailing stop from current prices depending on how we feel about the bet–

- If we think the **trend is coming to an end,** or some of our favourite indicators are flagging up a potential reversal, we can move our trailing stop much closer.

- If we think the **trend still has a long way to go** we can be more lenient, keep the trailing stop a fair distance away, and give the bet more room to breathe.

- If we have a **predetermined profit target**, when we reach that target we can move our trailing stop closer, rather than just exiting. That way, we preserve most of the profit we would have achieved if we just exited at our profit target, while still maintaining our position should the bet move still further in our favour.

There is one golden rule for trailing stops–

Once moved, they should never be moved back to a less favourable price.

Here is a chart of the recruitment firm Michael Page, which shows a trailing stop loss in action.

Figure 16.1: trailing stop loss, Michael Page

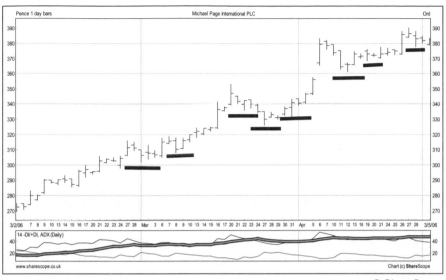

© ShareScope

An up bet was entered on 6 Mar 2006 (ADX reading over 30, DI+ greater than DI-, recent 2 month high, 4 day minor correction, and on the 5th day price exceeded the previous day's high). The entry was via a stop order at 310p.

- The first thick black line is the initial stop, placed below the low of the minor correction at 299p.

- On **8 March** a higher low was established, providing potential support.

- The initial stop was replaced on **9 March** with the first trailed stop just below this new low, at 306p (second line). The stock then really took off.

- On **22 March** a new higher low was established and the trailing stop was moved up just below this new low, at 333p, thereby locking in a move of just over 7% in this instrument (third line).

- The stop was hit on **27 March**, and the bet was over.

[But it was *au revoir* not *adieu*, as we will see in the next chapter on re-entries.]

Warning signs

A big move in our favour can be a warning sign that we should exit.

Surprising?

If, for instance, a stock moves 15 to 20% in our favour in just one day, the odds are it will subsequently need a period of time to absorb the move, so we might be better off cashing in and trying our luck elsewhere.

Further technical analysis

In addition to specific indicators and patterns that they use to generate entry and exit signals, most experienced spread bettors using technical analysis keep a watching brief on the charts of the instruments on which they have open bets. It takes a little while to build up your toolkit for this watching brief, but some of the tools you will come across as you explore technical analysis more deeply include:

1. **Indicator divergence**

   This is where the patterns on the price chart do not tally with the patterns in the indicator.

2. **Volume divergence**

   This is where the amount of trading in the instrument tells a different story than the price action. For example, with stocks, an upside break out is generally considered more likely to continue if it is accompanied by an increase in volume; if there isn't an increase in volume it is a warning sign that the break out may fail.

3. **Candlestick patterns**

   There is a wealth of information to be gleaned from interpreting candlesticks, a technique which goes back several centuries.

Imagine you are a doctor, and your open bets are your patients. They may look healthy, but you will want them to undergo a series of tests before you confirm they are OK. Technical analysis gives us the tools to conduct those tests.

We look at some of these topics a little more in the chapter on betting on reversals.

Example: exiting a trade, Reed Elsevier

In the meantime, here is an example featuring both indicator divergence and candlestick patterns. Learning to recognise these patterns is very similar to learning a foreign language. You start haltingly with a phrase book, and it all seems very difficult. With practice, it gets easier. Eventually you achieve a degree of fluency.

Figure 16.2: exiting a trade, Reed Elsevier

© ShareScope

An up bet on Reed Elsevier PLC had been entered on 29 Aug 2006: the instrument had made a new 12-month high, then pulled back for 6 days; the bet was entered via a buy stop on the 7th day when price moved up through the high of the 6th day of the pullback.

- 5 days into the bet, price reached a new 12 month high, and the trailing stop was moved up while keeping the bet open. Further gains were made and the trailing stop moved further up.

- Warning signs that the up move might be coming to an end were provided first of all by a divergence between the price action and the action of the 10 day Rate of change indicator (labelled Momentum on the chart). The price action was up, but the indicator was making lower highs. The thick black lines on the chart show this divergence, and the arrows point to occasions when a new 12 month high was achieved without the indicator achieving new highs. These warning signs were just that – not a signal to exit, but a warning to be vigilant, and keep the trailing stop close to the price action.

- A further warning was provided on 20 October when a bearish candlestick formed, a shooting star, where, after a rally, both open and close were near the bottom of a day with a wide trading range.

- The combination of shooting star and indicator divergence provided sufficient evidence to conclude it was time to close this bet without waiting for the trailing stop to be breached. *Bet over.*

- However even if those warnings had not been heeded, another was provided on 27 October when another bearish candlestick pattern called a Bearish Engulfing Pattern formed near the level of the top of the previous shooting star. This pattern is highlighted within the ellipse on the chart. This should have been a wake up call for anyone still long of the instrument.

Postscript

In this chapter we have looked at when to exit a bet, under four scenarios, covering adverse neutral and favourable situations.

Our spread betting account is now operational.

When we got stopped out of our bet in Michael Page we said it was *au revoir* not *adieu*. In the next chapter we look at what that means, when we look at the Re-entry.

17

The Re-entry

Sometimes, after we exit a bet, it becomes a good idea to re-enter it. This is what this chapter is about.

For less experienced spread bettors it can be a real wrench to exit a bet. It can feel like you have just lost a friend, particularly if this friend has been good to you and made you money. So, often they hang on too long, ignore the stop signal and end up turning a nice profit into an ugly loss.

It is a mark of the successful spread bettor that they exit promptly when they get the signal to exit, and then, if conditions are right, they are happy to re-enter the bet later.

Let's look at that graph of Michael Page from the last chapter once more. We had just exited our up bet on 27 March because our stop loss (at the third thick black line) was triggered.

Figure 17.1: re-entering a bet, Michael Page

© ShareScope

But on 30 March there is another buy signal: ADX above 30, DX+ > DX-, minor correction of 7 days, price rises above the high of the 7th day.

We are back in!

We place our initial stop below the low of the correction, then trail the stop as the bet starts working in our favour. At the right hand edge of the chart (3 May) we are still in the bet with our trailing stop fairly close to the current price.

So we were out of this instrument from sometime on 27 March to sometime on 30 March.

What did we achieve?

We protected ourselves in case that move down on 27 March was the end of the uptrend. We banked the profit that we had at that time, but that still didn't stop us from participating in the uptrend later.

Sometimes exiting and then re-entering an instrument costs us a few points. We are a bit worse off than we would have been if we had stayed with the first bet throughout. But those points represent well spent insurance.

In this case our technique for re-entering was to look for the same type of signal that we use to enter any other bet. In practice that is my preferred approach, However, like all aspects of designing spread betting systems, there is scope for modifying the rules, if we believe we can improve the system by doing so. Some spread bettors devise different rules for re-entry than for the original entry; for instance using more flexible rules for re-entry if the original bet produced a significant profit. For me, this is overly complicated. I stick with the same rules for entry and re-entry.

Postscript

This has been a very brief chapter, looking at one specific issue: how to re-enter a bet after being stopped out. We now have under our belt a strategy, betting on a trend, which can earn us money in our spread betting account. We could survive with this one strategy alone, and for many spread bettors – including myself – this strategy generates significantly over half of all their bets.

But it is useful to have more strings to one's bow, and therefore in the next chapter we look at the second strategy, betting on reversals.

18

Spread Betting Strategy II – Betting On Reversals

We have completed our look at Strategy I, betting on a trend. This chapter looks at another strategy: betting on reversals. We look at four techniques within this genre:

1. buying support and selling resistance,

2. betting on candle patterns,

3. betting on gaps, and

4. betting on divergence.

1. Buying support and selling resistance

As prices drop, eventually they may reach an area where we expect the fall to stop, an area where prices have stopped falling in the past. We can place an up bet in the hope that the fall will reverse. We are betting that a support zone will hold.

Similarly, as prices rise, eventually they may reach an area where we expect the rise to falter, an area where prices have stopped rising in the past. We can place a down bet in the hope that the rise will reverse. We are betting that a resistance zone will stay in force.

This is a safer strategy if the trend in a longer time frame is in the direction we are betting. If we are wrong in the short term, maybe longer term forces will still bale us out.

But not all support zones or resistance zones are equal.

Here are the factors that make a support or resistance zone stronger:

1. The **number of times support or resistance has repelled prices** in the past; the more times it has held, the more powerful it is.

2. **Volume at the support/resistance zone**: the more trade volume that has taken place at the support/resistance zone, the greater the number of market participants who will have a vested interest in the behaviour of prices at the zone.

3. The **wider the support / resistance zone**, the more likely it is to hold.

In general, the most obvious support and resistance zones are the best to bet on. You want them to be obvious so that other market participants act on them, like you.

The other key feature of support and resistance zones is that once broken they tend to reverse their role. A support zone once broken tends to become a resistance zone and a resistance zone once broken tends to become a support zone.

Here is a chart of BP from early May 2005 to early May 2006, which brings out some of these points.

Figure 18.1: support/resistance zones, BP

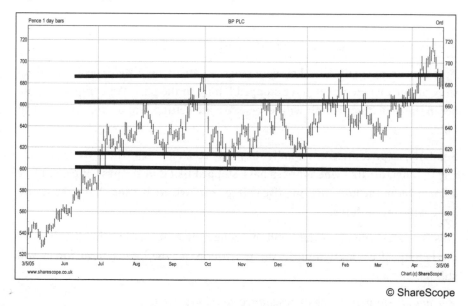

© ShareScope

The two lower thick black lines represent a support zone between 600p and 613p; the two higher thick black lines represent a resistance zone between 670p and 685p. At the far left of the screen we can see that 600p was at one stage a resistance area, but once resistance was broken it reversed its role and became support. This was seen on 26 August, when a fall in prices was halted. Between 19 October and 23 October prices descended once more into the support zone, but eventually the support zone checked the fall again. At this stage the support had worked several times and looked reliable.

up...

So, on November 11th, when prices once more reached the support zone an up bet was placed at 614p. The stop on this bet was placed at a point where the support could have been deemed to be broken, at 595p.

down...

By now the resistance zone shown by the two upper thick black lines had formed and taking that into account the up bet was closed on 23 November at 665p, and a new down bet entered.

up...

The down bet was closed slightly early at 614p on 16 December and a new up bet entered.

down...

This up bet was closed on 16 January at 665p and a new down bet entered.

out...

This latest down bet was stopped out since it looked like the resistance was being broken, although in fact it would have worked if held a little longer.

At the far right of the chart prices are currently above the former resistance area which is potentially reversing its role to become support (although this would be negated by a fall below 660p).

These bets illustrate what can be done if clear and effective support and resistance zones can be found. Up bets can be placed at support and down bets at resistance, and this can carry on as long as the support and resistance zones appear to hold. It resembles a game of table tennis with the ball being knocked from one end of the table to the other.

2. Betting on candle patterns

We looked earlier in the chapter on exiting our bet at how candlestick patterns can provide warning signs that a trend is running out of steam. The patterns can also be used to enter bets.

As we discussed before, it takes some while to learn to read candlestick patterns, but they are well worth the effort. The two books I have found most helpful in this area are both written by Steve Nison, and are referred to in Part Three.

A number of the candlestick reversal patterns tend to act as support or resistance, once formed. We have already looked at betting on support or resistance holding, and we can use these candlestick reversal patterns as a variation on this theme.

For this purpose I focus on a small number of patterns, the ones which in my own betting have been consistently profitable–

- patterns acting as potential **support**: bullish engulfing pattern, morning star, and

- patterns acting as potential **resistance**: bearish engulfing pattern, evening star.

It is possible to bet on many of the other patterns, but these are the ones I like.

Here is an example of betting on the potential resistance of a bearing engulfing pattern holding.

Figure 18.2: candlesticks, HSBC

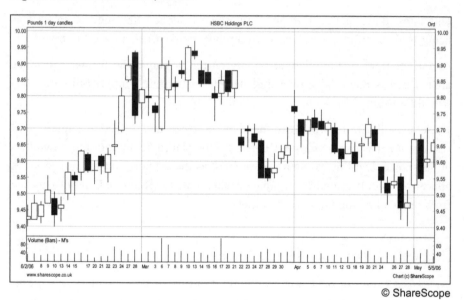

© ShareScope

- On **27 February** HSBC gapped up, and traders who were long of the stock were no doubt pleased.

- On **28 February** the stock again gapped up, but it was all downhill after that. By the end of the day HSBC had formed a bearish engulfing pattern, with the day's "real body" (the range between the open and the close) fully engulfing the "real body" of the previous day. Potential resistance had formed at the high of the two candlestick pattern, 994p.

- Four trading days later, on **6 March**, this high was tested again, and, betting that resistance would hold, a down bet was entered at 996p. A tight stop was placed at 1010p, just clear of the round number. There was one further test of resistance a few days later, but then the stock really took off on the down side.

- On **22 March** the stock gapped down, and this provided a subsequent opportunity for an additional down bet, which we look at in the next section.

3. Betting on gaps

Again, another variation on the theme of betting on support or resistance holding.

Gaps (also referred to as *windows* in candlestick terminology) are areas where there is no overlap between the prices within two consecutive time periods. Price has opened above the high of the previous time period and stayed above it for the whole period; or price has opened below the low of the previous time period and stayed below it for the whole period.

In the HSBC chart (p. 185), note in particular the gap that opened on 22 March: price opened below the low of the previous period (21 March) and stayed there throughout the period (22 March).

The area marked by the upper and lower boundaries of the gap, once formed, tends to provide potential support (if it is a gap up) or potential resistance (if, as in this case, it is a gap down).

Referring back to the HSBC chart once more, 8 trading days after the formation of the gap, price reached the upper point of the gap at 979.5p; betting that the potential resistance of the gap would hold, a new down bet on HSBC was entered at 980p, and the bet moved swiftly into profit.

4. Betting on divergence

As we saw in the recent chapter on exiting bets, classic indicator divergence occurs when price does one thing and the indicator does something inconsistent. For instance, price makes a new high, but the indicator fails to make a new high. In our chapter on exiting bets on a trend we used this as a warning sign that the trend might be losing steam. Indicator divergence can also be used to enter a bet.

Indicator divergence as a technique for entering trades gets a lot of press in technical analysis books and in some trading courses, but from a personal point of view I have not found it reliable enough for my trading style and risk preferences. Often the divergence is temporary, and the bet ends up losing money. I am happy to use it as a technique to exit, less happy as a technique to enter.

There is one exception, for me, one divergence technique which has produced a lot of profit. That is divergence in the Rate of Change indicator, for up bets only, using a fairly high setting (for instance 30 days). I look for price to make a new low and for the indicator not to make a new low. I then look for the indicator itself to form a bullish pattern such as a break of a previous high, or a trend line break, or the indicator achieving a three month high. This type of signal only occurs once in a while, and accounts for less than 10% of all my bets. But when it works it tends to produce relatively high profits, since in effect it gets me in right at the start of a new trend.

Here is an example which produced a profit, the FTSE250 stock GCap Media, which had suffered a major decline in price for an extended period.

Figure 18.3: divergence, GCap Media

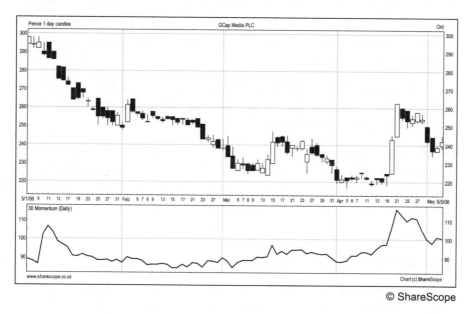

© ShareScope

- On 5 April GCap made a new low of 217p; but the 30 day momentum indicator at 88.577 printed a higher reading than its low for the preceding three month period of 84.558 achieved on 15 February, thereby demonstrating divergence from price.

- On **18 April** the momentum indicator reached a level of 97.03, higher than any reading over the preceding 3 months, generating a signal to enter an up bet.

- An up bet was entered shortly after the markets opened on **19 April**, at 225p (there was some minor slippage and this price was marginally higher than the day's high). A fairly wide stop was placed just below the three month low of 217p, at 216p. The bet was losing by the close on the first day but over the next two trading days the stock took off, rising to 262.5p.

- After a gain of over 16% in just 3 trading days, profits were banked the following day when the stock started to mark time. The exit was fine tuned looking at intraday charts (half hour charts).

Postscript

By the end of this chapter we now have two strategies for entering bets: betting on a trend, and betting on a reversal on reversals. Both of these strategies tend to result in bets which last a few days to a few weeks. In the next chapter we look at a different timeframe altogether, where we usually exit the bet the same day we enter it.

19

Spread Betting Strategy III – In And Out Within a Day

This chapter looks at betting on a very short timeframe – in and out of a bet within a day. You may already have decided that this is not for you, in which case skim through this chapter, just to get a feel for what some of the competition is doing.

You need the time to do this

Back in the dot com boom day trading became very fashionable, particularly in the US. Some Nasdaq stocks were growing exponentially, and people were giving up their 9-to-5 jobs to trade them. Some of them are now back in their 9-to-5 jobs – a little or a lot poorer.

If you are planning to make bets where you are in and out of in a day, bear in mind that this requires more time on your part than longer term bets. Some types of day trading require you to be at your screen throughout the day, and for many people this will seem like hard work.

Another important point about day trading: you will have to be significantly more skilful to profit consistently. Your average gain when you win will be much smaller than if you play a longer term game, but your spreads will not necessarily be much smaller. You will also almost certainly have to cover certain incremental costs such as intraday data.

With this proviso in mind, there are nevertheless certain situations where it is possible to profit from intraday bets. Particularly if you relax the traditional requirement that you have to close all bets before the end of the trading day, and as a result can hold a winning bet overnight to take advantage of further movement on day two.

Finding intraday bets

As always, we want to restrict our betting to situations where we have an edge. There are two ingredients here–

1. We will only bet in certain defined situations; we won't just take a punt because we think something should go up or down.

2. We are unlikely to be successful if we do not have access to intraday data.

Betting on opening gaps

An opening gap occurs when the prices at the open are beyond the range of the previous day, either higher than the high or lower than the low.

There are many opening gap strategies, both trend and counter trend. For example, bet that an opening gap –

1. is the start of a new move;

2. will get fully filled, prices will come back to touch the extreme of the previous day's range;

3. once touched, will provide support/resistance for a move in the direction of the gap; or

4. once filled, will start a new move in the opposite direction from the gap.

I use a variation of (4). I only look for opening gaps in the instruments which I have on my weekly shortlist for betting on a trend. I then look for a gap in the opposite direction to the current trend, and if the gap starts to get filled, use this as an opportunity to bet on the current trend reasserting itself. Because the gap in the opposite direction may be a longer term warning sign, I tend to use very tight stops on the bet, and also trail them aggressively, which often gets me out within one or two days.

Here is an example. We look at several days of action with the FTSE 250 stock EMAP PLC. There are two charts to look at. The first is a daily chart, the story begins on the day marked with an arrow, 23 November 2006. The chart runs up to 29 November.

Figure 19.1: opening gap, EMAP (daily)

© ShareScope

The second chart is a 15 minute chart showing the five trading days 23-29 November.

Figure 19.2: opening gap, EMAP (15-min)

© ShareScope

- No bets were taken on **23 November**. However the stock was on the weekly shortlist of up trending instruments (the ADX indicator was at 30 or above – as shown on the chart; and DI+ was greater than DI-, not shown). The lowest price recorded on 23 November was 821.5p.

- On **24 November** the stock gapped below 821.5p, opening at 820.0p and descending lower. Within just a few minutes price had got up to the previous days low, and the gap had filled. The stock moved up in price during the day closing at 834.0p. Although the ingredients were all there for a bet (stock trending up, a gap lower and a filling of the gap), this set up was all over before the completion of the first 15 minutes of the trading day, and only the nimble would have bagged the bet.

- As luck would have it, a second set up in this stock materialised just two days later, on **26 November**. The stock on this day gapped below the previous days low of 824.0p, opening at 819.5p and descending as low as 816.0p. Once again the gap was filled, as the stock rose to 824.0p; however, this time the process took longer giving the spread bettor more time to get organised to place an up bet. A bet was entered at 824.0p, with a stop just below the opening price of 819.5p, at 819p.

- **After just under a couple of hours** the stock had reached 838.5p, but then stalled for a while. This was an area where the stock had consistently stalled over the previous 7 or 8 days, and so, since this was only ever intended as a very short term bet, the bet was exited, at 836.0p. 12p profit, with an initial risk of 5p. – a 2.4 to 1 ratio (that's reasonable).

Betting as company results come out

Obviously, if we are betting on intraday movements we want the instrument to get moving after we have bet. It helps if we can predict that there will be a catalyst for a potential move. One such catalyst is the release of news for a stock; in particular the release of trading updates or results.

We can compile a list of stocks known to be releasing results – both Investors Chronicle and Shares list these for the following week. Then, on the day, we sit glued to our screens, monitoring the prices.

We want action, and we are probably going to get it.

One key point: it is not whether the results are good or bad that really matters, but what the market's reaction is to the results. The results may be fantastic, but if the market was expecting something even better the price of the stock may well fall. Similarly the results may be dreadful, but if the market was expecting even worse and everyone who was going to sell has done so already, the price will rise.

Sometimes the stock goes initially in one direction, then turns around and goes in the opposite direction. Just because the stock rises for the first two hours doesn't necessarily mean it is going to finish the day up.

But we will get action.

Our game here is to tune in to the direction the stock is going in the first couple of 15 minute bars then jump on board if it continues in the same direction, trailing tight stops during the day and jumping off if the trend pulls back to our stop.

Here is an example, the technology stock CSR.

Figure 19.3: trading company results, CSR

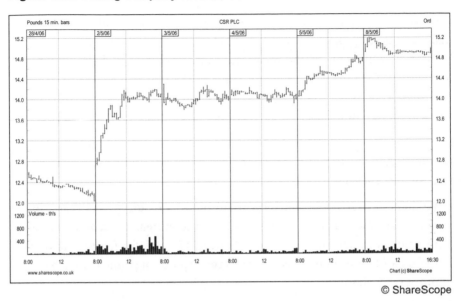

© ShareScope

On 2 May CSR, as scheduled, provided a trading update. Sales, market share and profit were all higher than analysts' expectations; as a result the stock was very much in demand. It was not necessary to know this to place a bet, the price action itself showed the way. Having closed the previous trading day at 1209p with a high for the day of 1258p, the stock got off to a flying start on 2 May, opening at 1273p.

- After two 15 minute bars, it was up to just under 1300p. At **8.31am** it cleared 1300p and an up bet was entered on a market order. It was clear that quite a few other people wanted to go long of this stock at this time, and there was some slippage on the order, which was filled at 1305p.

- The stock raced up to 1380p, then at **10am** it pulled back for about an hour, allowing a trailing stop to be placed at 1359p.

- By **11.30am** it had cleared 1400p, and after the short consolidation period which followed the trailing stop was moved to 1395p.

- The bet was held overnight, in case the stock moved further the next morning, but the trailing stop was hit before **8.30am**.

- The total move captured was from 1305p to 1395p, 90p, representing 6.5% of the purchase price.

Note: a few days later the stock continued its upward move without us; it is important not to get worried by that when one is betting on intraday movements as here; one takes a piece of the action and then moves on to other things.

Betting on false break outs

A break out above resistance or below support tends to get noticed by a lot of traders. A lot of people pile in, hoping to cash in on a new trend. But if there is no follow through to the break out, and price crosses back within the boundaries of the resistance/support, many of the traders who rushed in when the breakout occurred will be nursing losses and keen to exit. This can provide momentum to a price move in the opposite direction from the breakout.

If we want to bet on a false break out, it helps to try to stack the odds in our favour. Assuming we will observe the false break out on intraday charts, let's increase our chances of success in one of two ways–

- We look to have the **longer term trend in our favour**. We bet that a break out to the downside is false when the longer term trend is up, and vice versa; this brings us back to our weekly shortlist. We look for false break outs in the opposite direction to the longer term trend on instruments we have on our weekly shortlist.

- We look for **longer term support and resistance** at the same point as the possible false break out on our intraday charts, increasing the chance that if it is broken the break will be only temporary.

Here is an example of longer term support kicking in and enabling a bet to be made on a false break out.

Figure 19.4: false break outs, Unite (daily)

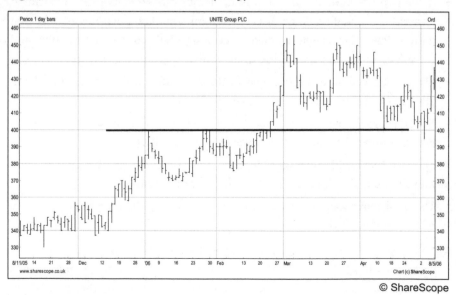

© ShareScope

Figure 19.5: false break outs, Unite (15-min)

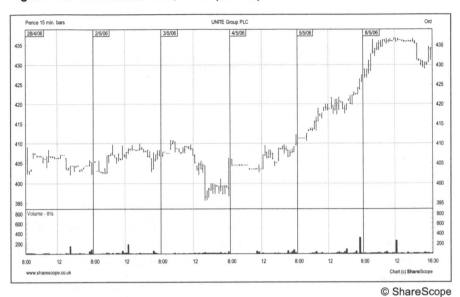

© ShareScope

First look at the 6-month chart. The thick black line shows that the round number 400p acted first as resistance and later, once broken, as support for this stock. Notice also that on 3 May price dipped below 400p but closed above it.

Now look at the 15 minute chart covering the period 28 April to 8 May. See how price dipped below 400p on 3 May just after 1.00 p.m. A break of major support such as this would have tempted some people to short the stock, but the attempts to short all fizzled out in a few hours.

Knowing that the longer term support was strong at 400p, a stop order for an up bet was placed at 401p. Simultaneously, a conditional stop order was placed as a stop loss at 393p (as protection should the up bet get filled). Business commitments prevented any possibility of following the stock's progress during the rest of the day (and in any case there was no need – the orders were in place, automated), but the up bet was filled during the afternoon. There was no artificial constraint that the bet had to be exited by the close of play even though this was essentially a very short term bet, so the bet was still open the next morning. After its brief foray below 400p the stock took off to the upside. Stops were trailed aggressively at roughly 1.5% below the price as it moved up, and the bet was eventually closed at 429p on 8 May.

Note: although this started out as a very short term trade, the trailing stops allowed us to stay in the trade for 4 trading days, taking advantage of the upside while continually managing the downside.

Betting on blow offs

Once in a while, everyone long of an instrument will head for the exits at the same time. This is often triggered by bad news, such as significantly worse than expected results. We see massive volume in the instrument and a massive drop in price. There is a commonly used phrase in the U.S. to describe this phenomenon – a *blow off*. Once everyone who wants to exit has sold, usually during one trading session, there is no one left to sell, and with no selling pressure the price rises. However after the first rally it is quite common for price to fall again as new buyers take profits, often getting quite close to (testing) the low of the blow off day.

One strategy to take advantage of a blow off day therefore is to enter an up bet when we believe the blow off is over, with an initial protective stop just below the low, trailing tight stops during the rally since we expect it to fail at least temporarily. Another strategy is to ride the instrument back down again as the first rally fails.

These types of bet are rare, but when they occur they provide the opportunity for huge gains. Here is one example from late 2004, the oil stock Cairn Energy.

Figure 19.6: trading blow offs, Cairn Energy

© ShareScope

Having been above 1500p only one month earlier, the stock had gradually drifted down to close on 16 December at 1362p. The next day it was announced that tests had been less positive than expected on a number of exploration sites and, as a result of this announcement, everyone headed for the exits simultaneously.

The stock opened at 1100p, down nearly 20%, and continued to drop during the first part of the trading day, reaching a low of 1003p. Volume was 10 times the daily average. But later in the day, when the selling frenzy subsided, the stock started to climb steadily. When it reached 1010p it looked like a blow off might have occurred, and an up bet was entered with a stop below the low (at 998p, just below the round number). The stock closed at 1115p for the day, but the up bet had been closed out a little earlier at 1110p, for a 10% gain in one day. It would also have been possible to place a down bet the next day as the rally petered out, although this bet was not taken.

Binary betting

The techniques we have already looked at in this chapter are potentially also relevant for both binary bets and fixed odds betting. However, these are different beasts from the ordinary spread bet, and despite their popularity have more limited application for the consistent winning spread bettors. This is for two main reasons: firstly, the instrument coverage is greatly smaller (only a small percentage of stocks covered for instance); and secondly, although the downside is limited so is the upside. Let's run through the various issues here.

Why are binary bets popular?

Binary bets have proven to be popular. Some of the popularity is due to their simplicity and their similarity to fixed odds betting. Fancy a bet? Grand National not on today? OK let's bet the FTSE 100 goes up in the next hour. The natural gamblers are in their element here, and the people who bet for fun or excitement. Serious spread bettors should only be looking to make binary bets if they think they have an edge.

With a spread bet, not only is direction important (i.e. will the instrument go up or down?) the size of the move is also important, since we potentially win more the bigger the move in our favour (or potentially lose more if we are wrong). With a binary bet, if we are right on our bet it doesn't matter whether we are right by a lot or by a little, we win the same; if we are wrong we lose our stake, it doesn't matter whether we are a lot out or only just miss the target. This is the simplicity of a binary bet, which many people find attractive.

Another attraction of both the binary and fixed odds bet is that they can be taken in quiet markets, when ordinary spread bets might seem unattractive. FTSE 100 dull and flat for the day, not showing any sign of trending? Then perhaps we can get the volatility we want from a binary bet or fixed odds bet, for instance that the FTSE 100 will close up or down on the day. The odds on these types of bet will be fairly responsive to small movements in the FTSE 100, and it is possible to trade in and out of the bets as the odds change.

Similarity to fixed odds bets

The difference between a binary bet and a fixed odds bet is mainly one of presentation. With a binary bet you bet an amount per point in the range 0–100; if you bet a certain event will happen you place an up bet paying the current ask price, and you will subsequently receive 100 if you are right and 0 if you are wrong. With a fixed odds bet you back a fixed stake. In both cases you are risking a defined amount to gain a defined amount. Some providers (e.g. binarybet.com) also allow you to bet an event will not happen; to do this you place a down bet on the binary bet, receiving the current bid price, and you will subsequently pay 100 if you are wrong and 0 if you are right. With a fixed odds bet you "lay" a fixed stake. With either binary bets or fixed odds bets you can trade long shots or the near certainties, according to your risk profile and temperament.

Common binary bets

Binary bets are most commonly taken on whether an instrument is going to be up or down at a set point, for instance the end of the day, various times of the day etc. Most providers allow entry or exit at any point before the set point for expiry of the bet. There are also many binary and fixed odds bets that can last longer than a day, they are not just for intraday betting, although they are commonly used for that.

Limited downside of binary bets

Some people are attracted by the limited downside of a binary or fixed odds bet – your downside risk if you are wrong is limited to your stake. Let's say you take a bet that the FTSE will end up by the end of the day. And it's being quoted at 49-54. You buy at 54, £1 per point. If you are wrong you will lose £54. Your downside risk has been limited to your stake. That's obviously different from an ordinary spread bet. It is much more like a call option. However, unlike a call option, where there is theoretically unlimited upside, with a binary bet your upside is also limited. Fixed by the odds when you took out the bet – you will get £100 if you win.

No doubt you will have spotted that the quote we have looked at adds up to more than 100. The chance of the FTSE 100 ending either up or down is not 105% clearly. So what is that extra 5%? That's an edge! Not for you, though.

Possible ways of getting an edge in binary betting

Here are some possible ways to try to get an edge in binary betting–

Take a punt

We could just take a punt. This is not recommended as a profit generating strategy, but that is what a lot of people do with binary bets.

Statistical edge

We could construct statistical models which show us that if, for instance, the FTSE 100 is up by 10 at 11.00a.m the chances of it finishing up on the day are X%, which in turn gives us an edge in assessing the binary bet providers' prices. There are people who do this.

Options models

We could develop an in-depth understanding of options pricing and construct detailed models for the binary bet market which enable us to take advantage of, for instance, changes in time value as the bet nears expiry. This also helps identify human error in the binary bet prices. There are people who do this – but they tend to be experienced options traders.

Arbitrage

We could try to exploit differences between the firms' prices through arbitrage. I suspect the spreads are too wide for this to be a viable strategy, but maybe someone has developed this approach.

Use our normal intraday strategies

We could use the same strategies as we use for intraday spread bets (e.g. gap plays, candlestick patterns etc). However, usually an ordinary spread bet will serve our purpose better, since we have seen that with correct use of stop losses we can limit the downside of a spread bet and keep the full potential of the upside, whereas with a binary bet upside as well as downside are capped.

Interesting developments in fixed odds betting

There are some interesting fixed odds bets available at a number of sites, including for instance betonmarkets.com. You can bet an instrument will (within a certain time period)–

1. touch a certain price

2. not touch a certain price

3. remain within a given range

4. touch two given prices, one higher and one lower

Opportunities to profit when instruments are range bound: you can bet they will stay range bound, or you can bet they will break out of their range.

Within these parameters it is possible to find low return high probability plays. For instance, with the second option above you can make a "no touch" bet which means you win if the price never gets to a certain point within a certain time frame. If you pick points well outside the current range you might find you can win 90% of the time, just making a small profit each time. You can create what looks at first view like a very impressive track record in this way. The problem is of course the other 10% of the time, when you might lose heavily.

To be a long term winner at fixed odds betting you need to factor in not only the number of times you win but also the relative size of your wins and your losses. If you are trying to develop an edge that is effectively built on the fixed odds providers getting their odds wrong, then be very careful, they are making profits and may not be as inaccurate as you think.

Postscript

We have now completed our look at the third strategy: in and out within the day. All three of the strategies we have looked at are directional bets, we are betting an instrument is going to go up or down. But there is another way. In the next chapter we look at delta neutral betting.

20

Advanced Strategies

It is possible to use spread betting in other ways than just to bet on whether an instrument is going to go up or down. Delta neutral is a term often used in options trading to refer to strategies which make money irrespective of whether the market goes up or down. In this chapter we look at delta neutral betting.

Arbitrage

Arbitrage involves buying and selling instruments simultaneously to take advantage of pricing anomalies.

Let's suppose that

1. one of our spread betting firms is quoting a daily cash bet on Standard Chartered at **1431p-1432p**; and

2. we notice that another of our spread betting firms is quoting **1438p-1439p**, which is out of line with both the market and all the other spread betting firms we have accounts with.

We could place an up bet with the first firm at 1432p; and we could simultaneously place a down bet in the same size with the second firm at 1438p.

Let's say that the price of the underlying instrument remains the same for the next minute, the first firm continues to quote 1431p-1432p, and the second firm corrects the pricing anomaly by now also quoting 1431p-1432p. We close out our up bet with the first firm at 1431p (losing 1p) and we close out our down bet with the second firm at 1432p (winning 6p). Total net profit for us £5 for every pound per point we put on the bets (presumably we loaded the boat) in about a minute. For zero risk since we had equal and opposite bets in the same instrument and therefore no exposure to any movement in the instrument.

Summarising this in a table–

Table 20.1: summary of arbitrage trade

	Time One	Time Two	Profit
Firm A quotes	1431 - 1432	1431 - 1432	
Firm B quotes	1438 - 1439	1431 - 1432	
Our action	Up bet with A at 1432 Down bet with B at 1438	Close bet with A at 1431 Close bet with B at 1432	Lose 1 point with A Gain 6 points with B

Welcome to the world of arbitrage!

In practice you are unlikely to have success at that game in any situation where the spread betting firms prices are based on an underlying instrument with a known current price. The reasons are straightforward–

1. For this type of game to be a winner you would have to cover the costs of the spreads (in this case 1p each for the up bet and the down bet, and in spread betting you probably won't).

2. You would need virtually instant execution of both the up bet and the down bet to avoid a timing difference which would cause you to have exposure to movement in the underlying instrument.

3. The size of the anomaly would have to be big enough to make a profit; in practice spread betting firms prices follow the underlying instrument closely even if the size of the spreads vary.

4. Where anomalies exist they will be very short lived (based on the relative speeds of the spread betting firms computerised response to movements in the underlying instrument).

5. You would need highly sophisticated software to be able to exploit anomalies within the required timeframe (likely to be seconds, rather than the minute in our example above). Such software does exist for trading in the underlying market but to my knowledge not in the spread betting world.

6. Certainly in the past, spread betting firms have not been in favour of their customers arbitraging in this way, and you may find you are contravening their rules when you look at the small print of your agreement with them.

Where there is no underlying instrument providing the framework for spread betting firms' prices, it is more likely that there might be arbitrage possibilities. Sports betting is the obvious example. Here, where there is more human intervention in the price setting, the possibility of pricing anomalies is correspondingly higher.

> From a personal point of view, this is not a road I have really wanted to go down. However, in the sports betting arena I am aware of a number of successful spread bettors who have made money through arbitrage.

Pairs trading

A loose form of arbitrage is pairs trading, which involves the buying of one instrument and simultaneously selling an equivalent amount of another (closely correlated) instrument. Overall you are neither net long nor net short, as losses you incur with one instrument are off-set by gains in the other. You hope to benefit from changes in the differential between the two instruments.

One established longer-term pairs trade exploits the differential between the price of oil and the price of gold. If oil becomes expensive relative to gold, you sell oil and buy an equivalent amount of gold, and if gold becomes relatively expensive you sell gold and buy an equivalent amount of oil.

The classic pairs trade identifies two instruments that have a normal price differential, where that differential has grown unusually large. The bet is that the normal differential will be restored, so you sell the stronger instrument and buy the weaker.

However, there is another way to play this on a short term basis, and that is to bet that the differential will in fact continue to grow, so you buy the stronger instrument and sell the weaker.

This second type of pairs trading when applied to stocks is popular with a number of successful spread bettors. Many pick two stocks from the same sector, looking at relative strength versus the sector. You buy the one with more relative strength and sell the one with less relative strength. If the sector as a whole goes up you hope the one with more relative strength will go up more than the other; and if the sector as a whole goes down you hope the one with less relative strength will go down more than the other. You don't mind whether the sector as a whole goes up or down.

If the sector moves up or down you will end up with one bet winning and the other losing. It is important to treat the up bet and the down bet of the pairs trade as being part of the same transaction. Don't look on the profit from one as a success and the loss on the other as a failure.

Over the page is an example from the electricity sector within the FTSE 100.

Example: pairs trade, British Energy v International Power

A good pairs trade in the period between August and November 2006 was to place a down bet on British Energy PLC and offset this with an up bet on International Power PLC. This left zero exposure either to the electricity sector, or to the FTSE 100.

Note that in the next two charts we show each stock's relative strength against the sector – this is useful since we want increasing relative strength in the one and decreasing relative strength in the other. An alternative is to plot the relative strength of one stock versus the other (which we will do shortly).

Figure 20.1: pairs trade, British Energy v International Power

© ShareScope

Figure 20.2: pairs trade, British Energy v International Power

© ShareScope

The relative underperformance of British Energy PLC, and relative overperformance of International Power PLC can be seen clearly during the period, with the thick black line on each chart showing relative strength versus the electricity sector.

Here is how this bet would have been placed at the beginning of September, at which point the relative strength of each stock versus the sector was apparent; the bet in effect was on the disparity of relative strength. To continue, let's assume £10,000 exposure to each stock.

- To gain £10k exposure to a *down* bet on **British Energy** PLC required a bet of £15 per point, placed at 676.5p at the open on September 1st (equivalent to £10,148).

- To gain £10k exposure to an *up* bet on **International Power** PLC required a bet of £32 per point, placed at 319.25 at the open on the same day (equivalent to £10216).

Note the small difference in exposure between the up bet and the down bet; this is due to only being able to bet in whole numbers of pounds per point.

As mentioned earlier one can also plot the relative strength of one stock versus the other; and this is particularly useful for monitoring the bet. One can look at the trend of the relative strength line itself, and exit the trade if the relative strength trend starts to break down.

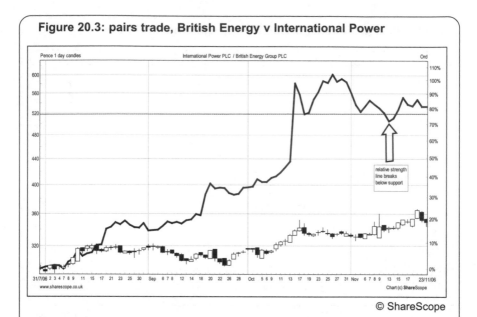

Figure 20.3: pairs trade, British Energy v International Power

© ShareScope

From when the bets were entered at the beginning of September the relative strength of IPR against British Energy initially showed a powerful uptrend. But the power of this started to dissipate at the beginning of November, and on 13 November the relative strength line dropped below previous support. This was a good cue to exit the pairs trade at the open on 14 November.

The actual outcome of this pairs trade (incorporating the spreads) is shown in the table below.

Table 20.2: summary of pairs trade

	Entry	Exit	Profit / (Loss)
International Power leg	Buy 32 pounds per point at 319.25	Sell 32 pounds per point at 341.25	704
British Energy leg	Sell 15 pounds per point at 676.5	Buy 15 pounds per point at 497	2692.5
Total profits			3396.5

It is important to remember that with this type of trade it is not necessary for both legs of the trade to be profitable, although in this case they were.

Hedging

Hedging involves protecting an existing position by taking an opposite position.

Why not just get rid of the first position?

Well, there may be all sorts of reasons why you don't want to exit the first position at this point in time. For example, there may be tax considerations. Suppose you have used up all your capital gains allowance for the year but are also sitting on a hefty profit from an oil share. Your long term view is that you want to keep the oil share, but your short term view is it is likely to go down. One game plan would be to sell the share now, wait for it to go down, and buy it again when it started going up again. The trouble with that plan is you increase your capital gains charge for this year, you pay stamp duty when you buy the share again later and you have commission charges on both your sale and your purchase.

A better game plan here might be to hang on to your share, avoiding the tax charges and commissions, and to hedge it. In the context of spread betting this would mean placing a down bet on the share with a spread betting firm equivalent to the amount of your share holding. As soon as you have done that you have no exposure if the share goes down - if it goes down the profit on your down bet offsets the losses on your share holding. If all goes well, when the share stops going down you will close your down bet with the spread betting firm for a nice tax free profit, and then you will be able to take advantage of all the further upside in the share holding.

The only problem with this second game plan is, if the share doesn't go down in the short term as you expected, you will have to close your down bet at a loss. That's a trade off you have to take into consideration when you hedge. Like any other spread bet you need to decide in advance when you will exit your hedging bet if it goes against you.

Postscript

This chapter looked at a number of ways of using spread betting other than in straightforward directional trades.

You have reached the end of Part Two, and you are now able to select from a range of strategies for spread betting.

We have been climbing the face of the mountain for a long while now. With a bit more effort we shall soon get our first glimpse of the peak of the mountain Spread Betting. Very few spread bettors ever get this far.

But, that first glimpse makes us realise we still have a long way to go. We have a spread betting account and we understand the mechanics of how to use it; we have had a look at a range of strategies for betting, and from those we have selected one, and have been getting on with it. Our objective however is more ambitious than that. It is the winning, not just the taking part, which matters here.

Part Three looks at some of the steps required to achieve consistent profitability.

PART 3

The Route To The Summit

Part 3 – The Route To The Summit

In Part 1 we reached Base Camp and equipped ourselves for spread betting. In Part 2 we started up the face of the mountain and reviewed a range of strategies for selecting bets. We have been climbing for a while now. Suddenly, in the distance we catch sight of our ultimate destination, the peak of the mountain. If we reach the peak we will be recording a consistent profitable performance with our spread betting account. But this requires more than just selecting some strategies off the shelf and expecting that to do the trick. Part 3 covers the other areas we need to take into account on our journey up the latter stages of the mountain. This is the part which losing spread bettors may find too abstract, and yet it is the topics here which will in the end do the most to turn a losing spread bettor into a winning spread bettor.

In Part 3 we look at matching the strategy to the individual; planningl record keeping; more risk management concepts; performance reviews, psychology – developing a winning attitude; and continual development.

21

The Right Strategy For You

There is a key element which every successful spread bettor has to factor in before choosing the strategy that is right for them – themselves.

It takes some spread bettors months or even years to settle down to a style of spread betting which enables them to produce consistent profits. You may have already come across people selling packaged trading systems which are promoted as the key to riches. It is actually very hard to bet successfully using someone else's system; at critical moments when full commitment is required to the system one's confidence in the system is likely to flag, producing a half hearted effort which gets nowhere.

But one has to start somewhere. From a personal point of view I have developed an eclectic style over a long period of time. When trying out new strategies I always start small, and build up over time if the strategies seem to work for me.

Here are some of the considerations which go into developing the right strategy for the individual.

Character

Different spread bettors will be more comfortable with some strategies than others. A closet buy-and-hold investor will find the transition to day trading more than a little difficult, and might prefer to look for bets that are likely to last at least a month. Someone who hates being out of the action might prefer a much shorter time frame where the opportunities to bet are frequent. Someone who hates giving up profits might not feel comfortable with a trailing stop loss and prefer just to exit on targets. Some spread bettors are only comfortable trading in an obvious bull or bear market when, if they are wrong, the market might still bale them out; and put their account into storage when the markets get choppy.

Then again, some spread bettors prefer to trade stocks, some are only interested in currencies. Others go for commodities. Some spread bettors like to look for opportunities across a wide range of instruments, others like to focus on a very small number. I know of one trader who traded just one German stock for several months. Nothing else. Got to know the movements of the stock inside out, and made a lot of money. Not for you? Fair enough.

The moral of the story is simple, you need to adopt strategies which fit your character and preferences. So you need to know what these are.

Account size

In one sense account size should make little difference if we all manage our risk in the same way. If we risk 1% of our account per bet, it means we risk £10 per bet in a £1000 account, or we risk £100 per bet in a £10,000 account.

There are some instruments however that we may not be able to trade with a small account. Take dollar sterling for instance: let's say our spread betting firm stipulates a minimum bet of £1 per pip. With a £1000 account, risking £10 per bet, we can only afford a bet where the stop is a mere 10 pips away. That probably rules out any bets on this instrument unless we make intraday bets. No problem, we will find another instrument to bet on.

Some people will find they trade better depending how much is in their account. You are puzzled? I know one person who does well with £5000 in their spread betting account, but seems to make a lot of errors when he has £15,000. They risk 2% on each bet. Somehow losing £300 seems a big deal, it puts them off, and have a string of losses; whereas £100 seems manageable and they win consistently. So what is the way round this psychological problem? Risk a lower percentage per bet as the account increases. Or the solution this person adopted, which is to reduce the size of the spread betting funds to £5000 each month, the size they were comfortable with. And bank a cheque for any excess.

Beliefs

Our beliefs about the market will influence the strategies we feel comfortable with. It is a valuable exercise to document our beliefs about the markets, to ensure that the strategies we are adopting are compatible with those beliefs.

Case Study 4

Simon had been spread betting for 15 months. He was marginally up in the first year and was comfortably up in the first 3 months of the second. But he was flitting from one strategy to another without really feeling settled with any of them. I suggested he should spend a little while thinking about and documenting his beliefs about the markets. Here is what he wrote,

"Markets trend

ADX is a valid measurement of strength of trend

Pullbacks are the best way to enter a trend

Bets should have at least a 2:1 reward/risk ratio

I like to trade with a system."

Not very much, and I noticed he had written at least another ten things down, but crossed them out.

We then looked at his ten most recent bets. None of them used ADX, none of them had a 2:1 reward/risk ratio, all of them were based on indicator divergence (which was one of the things he had crossed out). The strategies he had been trading had not been compatible with his current beliefs about the markets.

For the next couple of months Simon made systematic bets using ADX as a filter, looking for pullbacks in trending instruments only, and ensuring 2:1 reward/risk ratios were in place. Every other strategy was ignored for the time being.

To use a strategy to make spread bets we have to believe in it, and it has to be compatible with our beliefs about the market.

Do you know what your current beliefs are about the markets? Have you documented them?

Attitude to risk

Attitude to risk is important for spread bettors for several reasons–

1. It affects the basic decision to spread bet or not to spread bet. Spread betting involves risk, all the funds we place in a spread betting account could be lost, and more (due to the effect of leverage). Spread betting money is speculative money that should not be needed for any other purpose, and we must be prepared to accept the risk of putting those funds on the line. If not, we shouldn't be spread betting.

2. Awareness of, and respect for risk should be uppermost in our minds. We should manage the downside as the top priority before thinking of the upside.

3. We all have a different tolerance for risk. This is most obviously reflected in how much we choose to risk on each bet. For some people risking 1% per bet will feel right, others will prefer 2%, others wouldn't dream of more than 1/2%, and yet others will have to be persuaded that 3% is too much. And what about the ones that risk 10% per bet? They have been climbing the mountain with no support ropes and I am afraid they never made it to Part 3.

4. Different people will produce different results with the same strategy depending on their attitude to risk. Some will keep their trailing stops a little nearer than others, and get stopped out earlier, preserving as much as possible of current profits while reducing the opportunity for further upside.

5. Different people will prefer different strategies according to how they view the risks of the strategies. Does the risk of a loss seem low, but the corresponding gain also seem low? Or does the strategy seem high risk and high reward? Different people prefer different profiles of risk in their strategies.

It is not a simple matter of pulling a strategy off the shelf and getting on with it. We also have to put ourselves into the equation.

Postscript

We have reviewed some of the factors which make the right strategy for each spread bettor different, including character, account size, beliefs and attitude to risk.

In the next chapter we look at a key factor in spread betting success: planning.

22

Staying In Control – Planning

It seems to be a fairly common theme that successful spread bettors have good plans. We shed a little more light on this in this chapter, in two ways. First we look at what might appear in a successful spread bettor's plans. And then we look at a week in the life of a successful spread bettor, focussing primarily on planning routines.

The successful spread bettor's plans

These come in several forms: the annual trading plan, weekly trading routines, daily planning routines.

Annual trading plan

A good plan should provide a high level road map for the year ahead. It is generally easier to achieve something if you know what it is you are trying to achieve beforehand. Here are some of the areas that might be covered in the annual trading plan. Each section might be a typed A4 page in length, bullet point style. We are not trying to write elegantly in the plan, just get down the key points under the following key headings:

mission, objectives, goals

What do we want out of spread betting? What specific goals do we want to set? Here are some we might want to document: number of trades per month; win/loss ratio; ratio of average win to average loss; maximum peak to trough drawdown; maximum consecutive losers; return on investment; standard deviation of monthly returns; return to drawdown ratio; Sharpe ratio; cash flow; average profit per month. (Note we will examine these concepts a little more in the following two chapters).

strengths, weaknesses, opportunities, threats

Why do we think we can win (what is our edge)? Are we prone to any types of weakness? What are our main opportunities this year? What are the threats we need to guard against?

market selection, market directional philosophy, set ups, entries

What markets will we focus on? What is our broad approach to market direction (do we trade trends, if so, how do we define them; or do we trade counter trend; or do we prefer delta neutral strategies)? What main set ups will we use? And what specific entry techniques will we use with those set ups?

stops, profit taking, re-entry

What types of stop will we use (e.g. stops based on support and resistance, time based stops, indicator based stops) and how will we implement them (what algorithms will we use, will we automate them)? When will we take profits (e.g. at targets or using trailing stops)? If stopped out will we have a mechanism for re-entering the trade?

money management algorithms

How much trading capital will we have? What percentage of it will we risk on each bet? Will we pyramid?

risk management

How will we manage the downside? How will we diversify our risk (e.g. trading more than one market, using several trading styles, trading several timeframes)? What caps will we place on total exposure? How will we determine whether we should stop betting for a period (e.g. if we lose a certain percentage of our trading capital)?

beliefs

What are our beliefs about the markets? Are our beliefs consistent with the strategies we are planning to adopt?

trading and psychological rules.

What are the rules we will set ourselves? How will we know we have made a mistake (e.g. we could define any of the following as a mistake: not following the plan; not having a stop; risking more than 2% of capital on any one bet)?

trading routines

What weekly trading routines will we follow? What daily routines will we follow? What will we document? When and how will we review overall performance at spread betting – monthly, quarterly?

Weekly planning routines

We looked at weekly planning routines in Part 2. These centre mostly around preparing shortlists of instruments from which we will subsequently select our daily shortlists. Our weekly shortlists will reflect our trading methods. In Part 2, our example shortlists were of instruments with an ADX reading over 30, instruments outperforming or underperforming the FTSE 250 by 15% or more, and instruments making 52 week highs or lows. The shortlists are just lists of the instruments and should be held in electronic format, ideally using a portfolio function in our investment software.

Daily planning routines

Again, in Part 2 we saw that daily shortlists are prepared by identifying specific set ups that have formed on the price charts of the instruments on our weekly shortlist. The set ups should be recorded in electronic format; ideally, if we have software which monitors the markets in real time, using a portfolio function in that software. We need to record against the instrument the type of set up, the entry trigger point, the stop loss point which would be set if the trade is triggered and the initial profit target.

A week in the life of a successful spread bettor

To put some flesh on the planning processes, let's look at a week in the life of a spread bettor, Robert.

Robert has a robust annual plan, and mainly bets on UK stocks plus a number of commodities. He is so busy at work, it feels he has no time at all to plan his spread betting properly, but he has a set routine he has followed for several years, and is making money spread betting.

Friday evening

Robert downloads end of day data for his investment software at about 6.15pm. This takes one key stroke and then a few minutes downloading. Then it's out for the evening. (Quick check on the PDA at 9.00pm to see how the S&P 500 closed).

Saturday

Late start. Robert has a quick look at the charts of various stock indices, 3 US, plus German, French, Japanese, FTSE 100 and FTSE 250. He looks at charts of the UK market sectors. He then looks at the charts of oil, gold, copper, silver and platinum. He writes a couple of short paragraphs of what he has seen and compares this to last week's analysis. Not much has changed week on week. This week: mining and oil sectors are strong, as are all the commodities he follows. Telecoms (both fixed line and mobile) are looking weak, rest of the market patchy. This analysis takes about 30 minutes, including a short period reading a couple of market commentaries, one free, the other subscription based.

Robert prepares weekly shortlists from the UK 350 stocks, metals and oil. He has separate portfolios on his investment software for

1. ADX greater than 30, uptrend

2. ADX greater than 30, downtrend

3. Relative strength more than 15% better than FTSE 250

4. Relative strength more than 15% worse than FTSE 250

He goes through the 2 ADX portfolios from last week, and eliminates from them all the instruments that have ADX readings that have dropped to below 30.

Then he goes through all FTSE 350 stocks and the commodities he follows, adding to the portfolios any instruments where the ADX reading has crossed up above 30 in the week. The ADX portfolios take about half an hour to update, and he has about 35 instruments on the uptrend list, 20 on the downtrend. There have been about 10 changes in total.

He then goes through the 2 relative strength portfolios from last week and again eliminates instruments that no longer match the criteria and adds instruments that have crossed the 15% threshold. Again, about 10 changes, with about 25 instruments on each list. This takes less than half an hour.

Within an hour and half Robert has developed a good feel for how the markets have moved since the end of the previous week, and has updated his weekly shortlists.

Later in the afternoon he reads both of the weekly investment magazines to which he subscribes.

Sunday evening

Robert goes through his new weekly shortlists and looks for specific set ups that he trades. He finds only 4: 2 longs and 2 shorts. He goes into his real time monitoring system and puts the 4 instruments onto a watch list which will enable him to monitor the price action during the day. He notes the entry trigger level along with stop levels and initial profit target for each set up. He then goes into his spread betting platform and enters a buy stop order for each of the longs and a sell stop for each of the shorts at the appropriate trigger points, after quickly calculating how many pounds a point to bet on, in each case based on a stop 3% away from the trigger point. In total this takes about 20 minutes.

Monday

Busy day at the office. Able to check into real time monitoring system at lunch time, but nothing has happened. Not back home until 9pm. Check spread betting system. None of the orders reached trigger points at any time during the day. Cancels the stop orders. Does daily download. Analyses weekly shortlist for new set ups. There are none! Very rare.

Tuesday

Back home 8pm. Does daily download. Analyses weekly shortlist for new set ups. 8 of them, 5 longs and 3 shorts. Goes into the real-time monitoring system and puts all 8 onto a watch list which will enable him to monitor the price action during the day, if he can find the time. Notes entry trigger level, stop levels and initial profit targets. Goes into spread betting platform and enters a buy stop order for each of the longs and a sell stop for each of the shorts at the appropriate trigger points, and in appropriate size.

Wednesday

Despite best attempts, unable to find any time during work to check prices on PDA until after lunch. Discovers 6 of the 8 stops have been triggered! All 5 longs, plus one of the shorts. Calls up real time monitoring system on laptop, enters spread betting platform and puts sell stops on the new up bets and buy stop on the new short. Makes mental note to open an account with one of the firms that are offering automated contingent orders – that would have prevented the exposure through the morning resulting from having 6 new bets on with no automated stop losses. Back home 8pm., checks spread betting platform, the other 2 bets were not triggered, so cancels related stop orders. Daily download, usual routine, 3 new set ups. Puts the appropriate stop orders into the spread betting platform, and updates the real-time system with them. Records the new bets taken out during the day in the transaction log on his investment software. Checks all new bets to see if they have progressed to point where stops should be moved, they haven't.

Thursday

None of the new set ups reach trigger point, but 3 of Wednesday's up bets start motoring in the right direction. Robert discovers this in the lunch break, cancels the current sell stops on them and puts in new sell stops at the point where his trading methodology says a trailing stop should be established. With this methodology he now can't lose money on any of these 3 bets and indeed on one of them he has already locked in a 4% advantageous price move. One of the other up bets has had a poor time, and has been stopped out already. Later, the usual evening routine yields another 4 new set ups, which are processed in the usual way, ready for Friday. Updates transaction log with closure of the up bet that was stopped out. A check on the 5 open bets reveals that the current stops are all still in the right place except for the biggest winner which has now moved 7%, which requires the trailing stop loss to be moved another 1% up.

Friday

No new bets triggered, no stops need to be moved. It's been a quiet week. The application form to open an account with the firm offering contingent orders has arrived.

Postscript

In this chapter we looked at one the ways the successful spread bettor stays in control, through good planning. We looked at the form these plans might take, and monitored a successful spread bettor's actions over a week.

In the next chapter we look at record keeping.

23

Staying In Control – Record Keeping

Some of the pros say they can tell how good a trader is from the quality of the records that trader keeps. Certainly, poor records can be a symptom of a losing spread bettor.

We have already looked at the first type of record needed, the plan, which is a record of our intentions. The annual plan, the weekly plans in the form of shortlists, and the daily plan.

Also we need a record of the bets we have made. Some people just rely on the statements or the trading platform of the spread betting firm. For me, this is not sufficient. I record all bets in the transaction log of my investment software. This enables me to monitor performance in many useful ways, some of which we will look at when we come on to the quarterly review process. One of my rules is to always record a bet in the investment software on the same day as I make it. The software enables me to set up as many different portfolios as I want and then to aggregate them (in group portfolios). I have a different portfolio for bets based on each type of set up; I aggregate the portfolios in ways that I find useful. For instance, I have a different portfolio for bets made using each type of set up based on candlestick patterns, and I also have a group portfolio for all the candlestick pattern bets added together. I can create a graph of the profits generated from each of the candlestick patterns, and also of the total profits generated from all candlestick patterns. I can see how the profits from any pattern fluctuate; and if one type of set up appears to be performing increasingly well in current markets I can focus more attention on that type of set up, while focussing less on set ups that appear to be performing less well in current markets.

When phoning in bets it is important to keep a manual record of the bets entered, and then to check the spread betting firms statement when it arrives. It is fairly rare, but once in a while you might find a discrepancy, which clearly needs to be sorted straightaway.

To provide data for periodic reviews (and we will see how this data is used later) I personally find it helpful to keep a number of additional records–

1. A simple **trade spreadsheet** of data collected when I close a bet, showing the ticker code of the instrument, the type of set up used, the actual profit or loss, the percentage movement in price I obtained (plus or minus), and the number of days the bet was open.

2. On a **sample basis**, say one every five bets exited, a simple spreadsheet of the entry price, the exit price and the price after 1,2,3,4,5,10,15,20,25 and 30 days.

3. A **psychological diary**, recording the hopes and fears and emotions of spread betting. For the first 6 months of betting I made an entry into this every day, and learnt a lot by reviewing it later. Years later I still keep such a diary, but only make an entry into it when something relatively extreme happens. I am not recording what has happened in the markets so much as my own reaction to what has happened, so I can possibly learn from it later. I am particularly interested if I think I have made a mistake, or not followed my rules properly, since I want to find out later what went wrong, and how I can prevent it happening again.

Is this record keeping onerous?

It is one of those things which if it's done promptly every day takes only a few minutes; but if it is neglected for a while it seems hard work to catch up. The benefits become clear when we start to analyse the records to search for ways of improving our spread betting.

Postscript

We have been looking at record keeping in this chapter. In the next chapter we reap some of the rewards of this record keeping when we review our spread betting performance.

24

Staying In Control – Regular Reviews

In the last chapter we looked at record keeping. Perhaps your eyes were glazing over...? But courage! In this chapter we see what we can do with our records, and use them to improve our profitability.

It is important to review our spread betting performance periodically. What has gone well, what has gone badly and, most importantly, how we can improve our performance. One way to do this is to use the end of each calendar month as an opportunity to take stock, and undertake a more complete review on a quarterly basis. There are many different approaches possible, so you will need to work out what works best for you. What is important is to build in to our spread betting routines periodic opportunities to reflect on performance and to identify ways of improving it.

The rest of this chapter provides some pointers as to what might be in monthly and quarterly reviews.

Monthly review

Did we make or lose money in the month?

This includes all closed bets, with open bets valued at the current market valuation. The easiest way to get this figure is to simply lift the figures off your latest spread betting statements.

How much did we make or lose in the month?

As a percentage of our spread betting funds. Some people have cut off points; they bench themselves if they lose more than a certain amount or a certain percentage. This is to preserve capital and to have a rethink about what they are doing. Others adopt the same approach if they win more than a certain amount or a certain percentage. This is because in their experience they will otherwise get over confident and overreach themselves.

What is the trend of our monthly profits/losses?

Some people reckon that if they lose two months in a row it is time to stop, take the next month off, and go through the bets taken with a fine tooth comb and try to figure out where they went wrong. My software allows me to graph my profits for each portfolio and for each group of portfolios. So, going back many years I can see the equity curve for each set up I trade and for types of set up grouped together. I can see their performance ebb and flow as market conditions change. Importantly, I can switch more resources into the set ups that seem to be working best at the current moment; and switch resources out of the ones which seem to have temporarily dried up.

What is the cumulative profit?

Both in pounds and as a percentage on a rolling twelve month basis? If it is negative (i.e. a loss) then you should be keeping both the amount risked and your total exposure as small as possible until you acquire the skills and confidence to get the figure positive.

Other statistics to measure performance

I like to calculate the standard deviation of the last 12 monthly percentage returns, and I have a target for that standard deviation for my style of trading (less than 10%); if the standard deviation rises above 10% then that warns me I am taking on too much risk for my style of trading. I also have targets for the ratio of profit to maximum drawdown (maximum drawdown is the largest drop in equity from a peak to the time that that peak is next exceeded).

Quarterly review

Real learning and development should emerge from the quarterly reviews. The quarterly reviews take several days to conduct, including analysis of the data, time to reflect and developing appropriate action plans. They are very personal affairs, where you should face up to both the good and bad of your performance over the last quarter.

Note: For some people, it is easier to sit down with another person to go through their spread betting performance rather than to conduct the review on their own.

What you choose to examine in a quarterly review will depend on your level of experience, trading style, actual performance and strengths and weaknesses. Please note that to do the analysis required you will need to have collected the raw data. Here is a sample of things that might be included.

Performance of each type of set up over the period

Percentage of wins versus losses, average win size (% of equivalent value of underlying instrument), average loss (% of equivalent value of underlying instrument), ratio of average win to average loss, distribution of winners in various percentage boxes, distributions of losers in various percentage boxes, average holding period of winners, average holding period of losers (note if the average holding period of losers is longer than the average holding period of winners, you might well be cashing in your winners too quickly or holding on to your losers too long, or both).

Quality of exits

Compare percentage profit achieved on actual exits with percentage that would have been achieved by exiting all bets after 1,2,3,4,5,10,15,20,25 and 30 days. A real eye opener for most people when they realise that a standard exit after a set number of days might sometimes work better than their carefully managed exits!

Read through the psychological diary

Looking for patterns, themes, particularly looking at what was going on when any mistakes were made.

Progress against the annual plan

On track or not? Any new thinking which might be included in next year's plan?

Training and self development

Any books or courses that might help at this point? Or is it just more on the job training that is required to move to the next level of spread betting?

Postscript

This chapter has looked at ways of improving our spread betting through regular reviews of our performance. It is time to return to one of the key themes of this book: risk management.

25

Staying In Control – Risk Management

So far in this part of the book we have looked at improving our spread betting performance through understanding how the spread bettor must be factored into the equation, good planning and record keeping and periodic reviews.

But if there is one single thing to take away from this book it is that the successful spread bettors manage their risk better than the losers.

This chapter takes this theme further and looks at a diverse group of topics around the subject of risk management, starting with staying in tune with the markets, moving on to various aspects of position and exposure control (including the risk of over trading), and finally dealing with counterparty and contingency risk. A wide range of topics under one heading indeed. Bear in mind that trading firms have dedicated risk management departments addressing all kinds of risks, and we as spread bettors need the equivalent.

Staying in tune with the markets

Even for those spread bettors who focus primarily on UK stocks, it is important to have at least a rough knowledge of what is going on outside the UK and in other asset classes. We have at all times to stay in tune with the markets, because markets are increasingly correlated today. Here are four basic examples–

1. rising oil prices tend to help oil companies, adversely affect airlines;

2. a bull market in commodities tends to help mining stocks;

3. there is a correlation between US and UK markets, so if the DOW suffers we often see the FTSE suffer as well; and

4. falling bond prices (rising yields) are potentially bad for stock prices.

I find a useful way to keep a tab on relevant inter market trends and correlations is to subscribe to a newsletter written by a leading expert on the subject, John Murphy.

A top down approach works well for stocks. First, get an overview of inter market trends. Then look at the indices. Then look at the sectors. Finally compile a shortlist of individual stocks. Ideally, we want to find opportunities to place up bets on the strongest stocks in the strongest sectors in a rising market. And we want to find opportunities to place down bets on the weakest stocks in the weakest sectors in a falling market.

Monitoring positions

If you are day trading, you will probably be at your screen monitoring your positions for as long as you have any positions open.

If you are on a longer time frame, holding bets open from say two to thirty days, you will still need to monitor your positions during the day.

The least stressful way to monitor your positions during the day is to have automated stops on all of them; if your stop is hit you are out, if it isn't you are still in, and either way you don't have to be at the screen all day. However, there's a bit more to it than that. There are a range of situations which can occur during the day which might cause you to want to take some action before the close–

1. The instrument has a massive move in your favour, then looks like it is running out of steam – maybe time to cash in.

2. The instrument moves in your favour and you want to move your trailing stop loss in line with the move.

3. The market as a whole moves adversely for you and you also assess that the level of risk you are now carrying is too much for you; you decide you want to move the stop on the instrument closer to the current price.

So, although automated stops are valuable tools to control risk, and may often be sufficient, there will be some times when you need to check what is going on during the day.

As a general rule I try to check on prices a minimum of three times a day–

1. the first time about an hour and a half after the open (9.30am), then

2. in my lunch break (1.00pm), and then

3. about an hour before the close (3.30pm).

It is not always possible, it depends on other commitments, but this potentially gives me three opportunities to see if I need to do anything. I would say I leave everything alone and just rely on my stops 90% of the time. The other 10% of the time I am generally right in taking some additional action; however once in a while it becomes clear after the event that it would have been better to ignore what was happening and leave everything alone.

On the time frame most people use for spread betting, all positions should be monitored at the end of the day. The main types of actions we are looking to take are–

1. move a trailing stop if the instrument has moved in our favour and we wish to keep the position open,

2. tighten a stop order if we want to lessen our risk on an instrument, and

3. set an order to exit if we deem it is time to exit, possibly a limit order at a profit target.

Monitoring and controlling stops

In addition to moving stops on open positions, as just described, it is also important to monitor all existing stops held on our spread betting platform; this is a housekeeping task, but one that can easily catch people out-

1. Make sure there are no stop or limit orders still held for positions that have been closed.

2. Make sure that any stop or limit orders to exit current positions match the size of the current positions; this is particularly relevant if you pyramid positions moving in your favour; the initial stop will only cover the initial positions, and as you add to the position it is essential that the whole position is covered by automated stops.

Margin control

It is our responsibility to ensure we have enough funds (margin) in our spread betting accounts to cover our open positions. Most firms provide facilities to monitor this in real time. Most firms will send an email to alert a customer if the funds are too low for the positions that are currently held (a *margin call*); after that email there is usually a short grace period, but from that first email there is always the risk that the firm will start closing positions to free up funds.

Who would you rather close your positions, your spread betting firm or you?

The alternative to closing positions is to put more funds into the account, but you need to respond to that email quickly if that is what you want to do.

A margin call is a sign that something has gone wrong. You haven't been in control of your spread betting. Either you had too many positions open or they have gone badly wrong. Could be time to exit, take a break, review your spread betting and regroup.

Managing total exposure and leverage

Let us say we have thought through how much we want to risk on each bet, and have decided we will risk 1% of our spread betting capital on each bet.

How many bets can we have open at one time?

The answer to that question depends partly on our appetite for risk and our ability to multi task. If we are risk averse and find it difficult to move stops in the appropriate way when we are monitoring too many bets, then maybe we will set ourselves an upper limit of 5 bets open at any one time. We may not maximise our profits this way, but we will be staying within our comfort zone and within our area of competence. If things go wrong we will lose more slowly than if we were going full tilt.

But what is full tilt? How will we define our maximum exposure?

There is a well known formula that has been applied to a number of gambling scenarios, referred to as *Kelly's formula*. I am not going to go into a long critique of Kelly's formula in the context of spread betting, since for me it is partly a way of confirming a rule of thumb on leverage which has worked for me personally.

For reference, Kelly's formula got its first mention in a scientific article written by J.L.Kelly Jr. entitled "A New Interpretation of Information Rate" published in July 1956 in Bell System Technical Journal pp 917-926.

The formula has been used to identify bet size in some gambling games; for spread betting I use it as the first part of a two step process to determine maximum exposure.

Kelly's formula

The formula is:

```
K = (((B+1) * P)-1) / B
```

```
Where,
K = the "Kelly" amount, the amount to be risked
B = the ratio of the amount won on a winning bet to the
    amount lost on a losing bet
P = the probability of a winning bet.
```

Example

Let us say that I win twice as much on a winning bet than I lose on a losing bet; and that it is 50/50 whether I win or lose.

In this case K = ((2+1) * 0.5) – 1) / 2 = (1.5-1) / 2 = 0.25.

How I use the formula for spread betting

So in the first part of my process I reach the answer that 25% of my spread betting capital is the maximum in total I should have at risk at any time.

In the second part of the process I adjust downwards since the parameters I have fed in are variable not fixed.

OK, I have a track record of 2 to 1 average win to average loss, but that can fluctuate; and I have a 50% win/loss rate, but that can fluctuate. What if I am in the middle of a period where both parameters have dipped a little, albeit just temporarily? So I adjust the 25% down to 20% to allow for this, I cap my exposure at 20% of my spread betting funds.

If I am risking 1% per bet, this also caps the number of bets I can have open at 20.

What does that mean in terms of leverage?

Let's assume my risk per bet (both initial risk and risk via trailing stops) is usually between 2 and 3% of the price of the instrument, let's assume 3% taking into account slippage and spreads. Dividing my maximum exposure by my risk per bet (20/0.03 – 6.67) this means that, in this example, if I am at maximum exposure (with my risk tolerance and my trading profile) I will have exposure to instruments worth 6.67 times my spread betting funds. Rounding this down let's call it 6, and impose a cap of 6 times leverage on my spread betting. For most people, the appropriate figure is likely to be lower, in some cases much lower.

This calculation ties neatly into the age old wisdom that 5 or 6 times leverage should be the absolute maximum.

Driving the leverage car

It is a useful exercise to calculate the equivalent value of all your open bets, and compare them to your spread betting funds (i.e. to calculate your leverage). Here are some comments on various leverage figures you might come up with having done that calculation–

- **one or less**

  a good cap in your first year or if you have not yet learnt how to win consistently

- **two**

  too much unless you have started to win consistently, OK if you have

- **three**

  for many people this will be the maximum once they start to win consistently, depending on personality, risk tolerance, level of experience, track record, and profile of trading

- **five**

  you may well be close to overtrading even if you have a good track record

- **six**

  you are exceeding the speed limit, watch out

- **ten**

  the engine is overheating and the car can't stand much more of this; slow down!

- **fifteen**

  you have almost zero chance of survival; stop the car, take a break and regroup

Over-trading

Do you ever feel–

- You need to place a bet because you haven't placed one yet today, this week, or this month?

- You need to place a bet because the last one went wrong, and you want to get back even?

- Left out because you have no bet on?

- You're missing the action?

- You sometimes place a bet just for the sake of it?

If so, then it's time to step back!

It is OK not to place a bet.

It is OK to stand aside.

It is OK only to place a bet when you have a reason to.

Placing spread bets can become addictive, always be on your guard against over-trading. Winners are happy to wait on the side lines till the right bet comes along – one that fits in with their methodology. The methodology that is their edge.

Net long/short

We need to adjust our overall position in the market to match current market conditions. For instance, if we have multiple stock bets open it is important to know how we would stand, net long or net short, if we held the equivalent value of the underlying instruments. In a raging bull market we might go 100% long and in a powerful bear market we might go 100% short, but in most other market conditions we will try to get somewhere between these two extremes.

Diversification

We are not aiming, like a long term investor, to build up a carefully balanced and diversified portfolio of positions. But we should be trying to avoid making a series of bets that are just like one big bet that would exceed our limits on the amount we want to risk on any one bet.

Let's say we have five open bets including three long bets, one on Xstrata, one on Anglo American, one on BHP Billiton. That's not very different from just having one big bet on Anglo American. They are all miners, they all respond to movements in certain commodity prices, they are highly correlated. Let us say we now have two new potential up bets, one on Lonmin, another miner, another on CSR, a technology company. It might be time to have a go at something outside the mining sector?

Standing aside

A consistent theme in this book – it is always OK to stand aside.

I know several successful spread bettors who as a matter of routine stand aside every couple of months, even if it is just for a few days. No new bets for a little while, closing down the open positions – a period of stillness, away from the markets. They come back refreshed and are able to start again with a clear mind. Good times to stand aside, at least briefly, are after a losing month (to regroup), after a huge winning month (because overconfidence seems to lead inevitably to underperformance), or when you have something major happening in your life (which will prevent you from giving your spread betting due care and attention).

And holidays – close everything down and take a well earned rest!

Counterparty risk

What happens if your spread betting firm goes bust?

In theory the customer funds should be segregated, and you should be able to get your money back, subject to maxima applicable in current legislation. In practice, I prefer to split my spread betting funds over several accounts. I also draw funds out of them when they reach certain predefined values and put the money to use elsewhere.

Exceptional events

There is always the risk of an exceptional event. You can be short an instrument and a take over bid is tabled. You can be long an instrument and war breaks out. In these circumstances the markets will go wild and even if you have automated stops you will suffer extreme slippage on them and lose far more than you had budgeted for.

That is one of the dangers of extreme leverage. You will get hurt far more when an exceptional event occurs.

Potentially greater risk, but also potentially greater reward. I have been long several times when a takeover bid produced exceptional profits.

If you want to play this game, you have to live with the risk of exceptional events. If you can't stand the thought of the risk then maybe the game isn't for you.

To manage the risk as best we can, we keep bet sizes, total exposure and our net long/short position at appropriate levels, and automate our stops.

Contingency planning

Certain events that might cause us big problems we can think through in advance, and try to develop contingency plans to deal with those events. The events may be local to us rather than being world events. As an example I have contingency plans to cope with such things as:

- a power failure,

- my laptop malfunctioning,

- serious illness/incapacity (do you really want your spread bet positions open while you are in hospital?),

- a skewed distribution of winners/losers, and

- a unique catastrophic market event.

The plans may not be perfect, but at least I have thought through my responses to these situations.

Postscript

This has been a long and complex chapter, on a complex but critical subject. It covers an area that winning spread bettors are good at. Losing spread bettors can have winning streaks, but if they don't manage risk properly sooner or later they will implode, never to be seen again.

In the next chapter we look at developing a winning attitude and profile the successful spread bettor.

26

Developing A Winning Attitude

Spread betting is a difficult game. We learn the mechanics, we find set ups that work for us, we implement our set ups efficiently when they are triggered, we manage our risk, we use appropriate money management, we stay in tune with the markets. But two people with equal skills in all these areas will still produce different results.

A small digression into professional golf (or your favourite sport): top golfers all have unbelievably good technique, but the consistent winners seem to be able to raise their game when it matters.

At spread betting it takes some while to get to the stage where consistent profits are achieved. Many people never get that far. The ones that do have mastered something more than the techniques of the game itself. They have mastered themselves and have developed a winning attitude to the game.

It's hard to think of a sensible short cut, since part of the winning attitude comes from having a track record of...winning.

Success breeds success.

More than most other games, spread betting is about cutting down on errors and managing the downside. In cricketing terms it is about staying at the crease and defending your wicket rather than trying to hit runs. Once in a while you will get a loose ball that you can hit for four, and there will be plenty of safe singles, but you have to stay in to get that opportunity.

You will be offered many alleged short cuts and "secrets of the game" as you try to improve your spread betting results. The only secret is that there is no secret. The markets themselves are, in the long run, our teachers, and we have to serve our time as their pupils.

Winning spread bettors that are able to call up a graph of their spread betting profits over the years can often find a point in time when the slope of the graph turned up, or more up, a defining moment when they seemed to come of age as a spread bettor. That defining moment will have been triggered by different things for different people. Maybe a book, maybe a course, maybe a certain market experience in a series of market experiences, or maybe something outside of trading.

From a personal point of view one of the most helpful books I have ever read on this subject is the book by Mark Douglas referred to in the next chapter. You might also find the www.iitm.com web site interesting.

This chapter concludes with a profile of the successful spread bettor.

Profile of the successful spread bettor

Successful spread bettors are quite distinctive; winners have a quite different approach to losers, which includes-

1. having an edge,

2. positive expectancy,

3. having a game plan,

4. being in control, and

5. assuming responsibility.

1. Having an edge

Winners have an edge that is personal to them. They know what it is and they exploit it – methodically. They can define their edge, and when their edge is available they act on it. An edge might be an in-depth knowledge of a stock sector, or mastery of a technical analysis indicator, or a particular trading system based on directors dealing. But note that an edge that works successfully for one person may be totally unsuitable for another.

To find an edge that is right for you is not an overnight task. It takes time to develop an edge and it is hard work, a process of trial and error that involves taking some knocks on the way. As well as developing methods that work it also crucially involves developing methods that fit your personality and your own personal risk profile.

Summary: if you don't have an edge – and recognise clearly what that edge is – you won't make money spread betting.

2. Positive expectancy

Winners have a positive expectancy that is derived from their edge. In effect they can quantify their edge. For a particular methodology they will know–

1. the expected percentage of wins versus losses,

2. the average size of a win, and

3. the average size of a loss.

From this they can derive their profit expectancy.

For example, let us say that a methodology produces on average 6 winning bets for every 4 losing bets; that for every £100 invested via this methodology the average win for the 6 winners will be £10 and the average loss for the 4 losers will be £5. Then the expected outcome will be (60% x £10) minus (40% x £5) which comes to £4 profit for every £100 invested via this methodology. That is a positive expectancy (i.e. we will expect to win over the long run with this methodology). We just keep on acting on our edge that gives us a positive expectancy, over and over again, and let the probabilities work in our favour.

The two routes to positive expectancy are–

1. Show often we win, and

2. the relative size of our wins versus the relative size of our losses.

What we feel comfortable with will depend a lot on us. Some people prefer to develop an edge that generates a high percentage of winners; others are comfortable with a much lower percentage of winners, provided their average win size is way more than their average loss size.

To shed a bit more light on this at this point: many of the most successful spread bettors operate with not much more than 50% of their bets winning. It is perfectly possible to be successful with as little as 40% of your bets winning – provided you keep the wins relatively big and the losses relatively small.

> I personally like to use methodologies that win about 60% of the time, and that is right for me, but there are many configurations of this formula.

Many successful spread bettors target for their wins to be on average at least 3 times as big as their losses, and in practice end up with well over 2 times. You have to develop an edge that is right for you. The edge has to fit your own personal risk profile.

Spread betting is a game of chance where you try to stack the odds in your favour and then wait for the law of averages to play itself out. With positive expectancy you will win in the long run although the outcome of any one bet cannot be predicted.

3. Having a game plan

Winners have good plans. Plans of every shape and size. Long term plans, short term plans, written trading plans, exit plans – you name it, they have got it planned. It is no accident that they win. They have worked out how to win in their plans: they carry out their plans, then they review what they have done after the event to see whether there is anything to learn, to put in to their future plans.

OK, it's an old cliché, but apt none the less–

winners plan the trade then trade the plan

4. Being in control

Winners know that the outcome of any particular trade cannot be known. But whatever can be controlled in the process, winners control: from planning, through to implementation of the bet, through to monitoring, through to post bet evaluation. Winners seem to be in control of their destiny.

5. Assuming responsibility

Each spread bettor needs to come face to face with the truth that whatever happens in their spread betting account is down to them. The power to succeed or fail rests entirely with them. It is a mark of successful spread bettors that they have come to terms with this truth.

10 Rules for Profitable Spread Betting

For those that like things summarised in rules, here are 10 that capture the essence of winning at this game–

1. Have written plans and rules
2. Never bet without an edge
3. Only use methods that suit you
4. Understand the rewards, risks and odds of your methods
5. Stay in control of your betting and yourself
6. Focus on planning your exits
7. Don't bet too much on any one bet, or in aggregate
8. Stay in tune with the markets
9. Monitor your performance, and adapt
10. Accept it is down to you and no one else

Postscript

In this chapter we have looked at developing a winning attitude, and profiles the successful spread bettor. In the next chapter we look at continual development.

27

Continual Development

Books

These are the 25 books (out of several hundred) in my library that I believe have had the biggest impact on my own spread betting performance:-

Inter market analysis

John J. Murphy: *Intermarket Analysis: Profiting from Global Market Relationships* (John Wiley & Sons Inc., 2004)

Technical analysis

John J. Murphy: *The Visual Investor: How to Spot Market Trends* (John Wiley & Sons Inc., 1996)

John J. Murphy: *Technical Analysis of the Financial Markets: A Comprehensive Guide to Trading Methods and Applications* (New York Institute of Finance, 1999)

Introductions to trading

Dr. Alexander Elder: *Trading for a Living: Psychology Trading Tactics Money Management* (John Wiley & Sons Inc., 1993)

Dr. Alexander Elder: *Come into my Trading Room: A Complete Guide to Trading* (John Wiley & Sons Inc., 2002)

Developing trading systems

Tushar S. Chande: *Beyond Technical Analysis: How to Develop and Implement a Winning Trading System* (John Wiley & Sons Inc., 2001)

Bruce Babcock Jr.: *The Business One Irwin Guide to Trading Systems* (Business One Irwin, 1989)

Charles Le Beau & David W. Lucas: *Technical Traders Guide to Computer Analysis of the Futures Market* (McGraw-Hill 1992)

Trading issues such as position sizing

Van K. Tharp: *Trade Your Way to Financial Freedom: Van Tharp's Secrets to Searching for the Holy Grail in the Market, Finding a Trading System that Works for You, Selecting a Timeframe and Market* (McGraw-Hill, 1999)

Psychology and trading

Mark Douglas: *Trading in the Zone: Master the Market with Confidence, Discipline and a Winning Attitude* (New York Institute of Finance, 2000)

Interviews, autobiographies, biographies

Jack D. Schwager: *Market Wizards: Interviews with Top Traders* (Harper Business, 1989)

Jack D. Schwager: *The New Market Wizards: Conversations with America's Top Traders* (Harper Business, 1992)

Jack D. Schwager: *Stock Market Wizards: Interviews with America's Top Stock Traders* (John Wiley & Sons Inc., 2001)

Nicholas Darvas: *How I Made $2,000,000 in the Stock Market* (Harriman House, 2007)

Edwin Lefevre: *Reminiscences of a Stock Market Operator* (John Wiley and Sons, Inc., 1993, originally published in 1923 by George H. Doran and Company)

Specific techniques

J. Welles Wilder Jr.: *New Concepts in Technical Trading Systems* (Trend Research, 1978)

Steve Nison: *Japanese Candlestick Charting Techniques: A Contemporary Guide to the Ancient Investment Techniques of the Far East* (New York Institute of Finance, 2001)

Steve Nison: *Beyond Candlesticks: New Japanese Charting Techniques Revealed* (John Wiley & Sons Inc., 1994)

John Bollinger: *Bollinger on Bollinger Bands* (McGraw-Hill, 2002)

Jeremy du Plessis: *The Definitive Guide to Point and Figure: A Comprehensive*

Guide to the Theory and Practical Use of the Point and Figure Charting Method (Harriman House Publishing, 2005).

Set ups

Laurence A. Connors: *Advanced Trading Strategies* (M. Gordon Publishing Group, 1998)

David Landry: *Dave Landry on Swing Trading* (M. Gordon Publishing Group, 2002)

Jeff Cooper: *Hit and Run Trading: The Short-Term Traders' Bible* (M. Gordon Publishing Group, 1996)

Jeff Cooper: *Hit and Run Trading II: Capturing Explosive Short-Term Moves in Stocks* (M. Gordon Publishing Group 1998)

Laurence A. Connors & Linda Bradford Raschke: *Street Smarts: High Probability Short Term Trading Strategies* (M. Gordon Publishing Group, 1995)

Courses

There are many courses out there: on short term trading; on technical analysis; on spread betting. Some good value and some less so. I would strongly recommend you get feedback from previous participants before signing up to any of the really expensive ones.

They can broadly be categorised by price–

1. Freebies: introductions by spread betting firms to their products and services, or tasters for the really expensive courses where you get a couple of hours free tuition to see what you might get if you make a purchase. These are fine, but you may get quite a strong sales pitch at the end. Don't go along if you are the sort of person that might sign up just to avoid embarrassment.

2. Minimally priced short seminars at exhibitions and conferences; can be of value to the less experienced spread bettor.

3. Short seminars run by magazines such as Investors Chronicle; usually good value especially in the early days of trading.

4. Low to medium priced courses: these tend to cost between £250 and £650 for a day, depending on what is being taught and the credentials of the tutors. There are several good value courses out there, but talk to previous attendees, or read any articles or books the tutors may have written, to assess whether the course might be of value to you.

5. High priced courses: these are often 2 or 3 day events priced anywhere from £1500 to £5000, although you may well encounter time-honoured marketing techniques such as special discounts for early booking, so it might appear you are saving £1000 or more. Let common sense prevail. Check out the credentials of the tutors, get feedback from previous attendees, do a cost benefit analysis and consider alternatives. If your spread betting account is only £3000 for instance, does spending £3000 on a course really make sense? Maybe you would be better off buying a dozen good trading books. And remember, more expensive doesn't necessarily mean better.

Magazines

The weekly investment magazines from time to time carry articles or have special features of interest to spread bettors. For instance, on trading strategies, products, courses, books etc., as well as providing general background information on the markets. The monthly magazine *Traders'* is produced specifically for short term traders and is of great interest to spread bettors.

Web sites

We have looked at many web sites during the course of this book. By the time you read this book, there will no doubt be several new and valuable sites to explore.

The final postscript....

So, maybe now we can just catch sight of the path to the peak of Spread Betting mountain. Congratulations for staying the course. We are not quite there yet, but maybe as we strive for continual improvement we may get a little closer.

To quote from one of my all time favourite books–

> *"Despite our constant pursuit of knowledge, the market itself assures there is no shortcut to obtaining our final degree. In the end, it is experience which is our ultimate teacher and there is no substitute. We can only choose the attitude with which we approach this process of learning to trade."*

Street Smarts: High Probability Short Term Trading Strategies, Laurence A. Connors & Linda Bradford Raschke

Appendix

This appendix is intended to provide supplementary information on a number of subjects which could not conveniently be covered in the body of the text.

Examples of Basic Bets

This is not a beginners book, but a few examples of basic bets are included for anyone that feels it would be useful to go over these as background reading. Most of the firms include such examples in their marketing material and on their websites.

Example 1

- October FTSE 100 is quoted at 5950p-5954p.

- You think FTSE 100 is going down, so you sell October FTSE 100 at 5950p £2 per point.

- Three weeks later October FTSE 100 is quoted at 5880p-5884p.

- You think FTSE 100 is due for a rally now and you decide to exit your bet. You buy October FTSE 100 at 5884p £2 per point which closes your open position.

- You have made a profit of £132 (5950p-5884p times £2).

Example 2

- Vodafone rolling daily bet is quoted at 124.25p-124.5p.

- You think Vodafone is oversold and is due to rally now. You buy Vodafone rolling cash at 124.5p for £100 per point.

- After 4 days Vodafone no longer looks like it's going to rally and you no longer want to be long of it. The latest quote on the rolling daily bet is 122.25-122.5 and you sell Vodafone rolling cash at 122.25p for £100 per point which closes your open position.

- You have made a loss of £225 (124.5p-122.25p times £100), *plus* the overnight interest you have been charged on the bet over the 4 days (reflected in adjusted opening positions each day) which comes to about £9.

Example 3

- The binary bet for FTSE 100 to be up on the day is trading at 55-60.

- You believe it will close up, and take out a bet at £10 per point, buying at 60.

- You are aware that if the FTSE does not close up on the day the binary bet will be valued at 0, i.e. you will lose £600 (0-60 x £10); but if it does close up on the day the binary bet will be valued at 100, i.e. you will win £400 (100-60 x £10).

- At 4.00 p.m. FTSE is struggling a few points below break even for the day and the binary bet is now priced at 58-63. You decide the risk of holding on is not worth it, so you close your bet, selling at 58, for a loss of £20 (58-60 x £10).

Example 4

- October Barclays (a futures style bet) is quoted at 600-604.

- You believe Barclays is heading down and you open a bet, £10 per point, selling at 600.

- On 6 October, having held the bet for 5 weeks, you decide that the downtrend which you correctly predicted is not going to last until expiry (with your spread betting firm expiry is on the third Wednesday of the contract month), so you check the price and find October Barclays quoted at 577-580.

- You buy for £10 per point at 580, closing your open position, and making £200 profit (600-580 x £10).

Spread Betting Glossary

Spread betting terms (and trading terms) are not always clear or consistent. This list is not designed to be in any way comprehensive, but will hopefully clarify some of the jargon for some people.

ask price	see *offer*
bid price	The price at which the spread betting firm / market maker buys and you sell
buy	You profit if the instrument goes up (see: *up bet*, *long*)
contingent orders	(also called **if done orders**): a mechanism by which first a stop or limit order is placed; then, if and only if the order is triggered, a second order is automatically set against the new position
controlled risk bet	A bet where the maximum loss is predefined (i.e. a bet with a guaranteed stop loss)
cover	To exit or buy back a short position
down bet	A bet where you profit if the instrument goes down (see *sell, short*)
fill	Where your order is executed
futures style bets	bets structured like a futures contract, generally expiring at the next quarter ("near month") or the quarter after that ("far month"). Some longer futures style bets now in existence, expiring 9 months or a year out
guaranteed stop loss	A stop loss where you are guaranteed to an exit price (i.e. the key feature of a controlled risk bet)
if done orders	see *contingent orders*
LIBOR	London inter-bank offered rate, a short term interest rate set by the Bank of England often used by spread betting firms as a base for calculating finance charges for futures style bets

limit order	An order to buy or sell if the market reaches a specified price that is more favourable than the current price
long	You profit if the instrument goes up (see *buy*, *up bet*)
margin	The amount of money you need in your account to keep a bet open
margin call	Where you are advised by the spread betting firm that you need to put more money into your account to fund your open bets
OCO orders (One Cancels the Other)	Mechanism for placing two orders at the same time, one above and one below the market; if one is triggered then the other is cancelled
offer (offer price)	The price at which the spread betting firm / market maker sells and you buy; sometimes referred to as the ask or asking price
pounds per point	The usual way of describing the size of a bet; for instance with UK shares one point equals one penny so if you bet one pound per point you gain or lose one pound for every penny the share moves
rollover	The closing of an open bet and the opening of a new bet for the same amount at a point in time; typically incurs a charge for futures style bets
sell	You profit if the instrument goes down (see *down bet*, *short*)
short	You profit if the instrument goes down (see *sell*, *down bet*)
spread	The difference between the bid and the offer price
stop / stop loss	An order to buy or sell at a price that is less favourable than the current price; mainly used to limit risk
up bet	You profit if the instrument goes up (see *buy*, *long*)

ADX

I like this indicator, and in my view it deserves as much coverage as its better known relatives, such as RSI (out of the same stable). I refer to ADX on a number of occasions and therefore provide a little additional information on it here.

The Average Directional Movement (ADX) was first presented in Welles Wilder's book, *New Concepts in Technical Trading Systems* (Trend Research, 1978). The calculations are quite complex, but the concepts fairly straightforward. Simply put, directional movement is that part of a price bar which is outside the previous price bar's range.

Using a daily price bar as an example,

- **positive** directional movement (DM+) is the price action that is above yesterday's high,

- **negative** directional movement (DM-) is the price action that is below yesterday's low.

Inside days (today's range is within yesterday's range) are assumed to have zero directional movement. Outside days (today's high is higher than yesterday's high and today's low is lower than yesterday's low) are deemed to have either positive or negative directional movement (not both) depending on which is larger. Any gaps up or down are included in the relevant DM+ or DM- calculations.

To be able to compare directional movement across instruments with varying prices DM+ and DM- are divided by the range of today's price action (including any gaps) converting all action to a 0 to 100 scale.

To smooth the data an average is taken over a series of days, usually between 10 and 18, the most common being 14. These averaged figures are usually referred to as DI+ and DI-. Again, the smoothed figures will lie on a scale between 0 and 100. A high DI+ figure will indicate strong positive directional movement over the period, a high DI- figure will indicate strong negative directional movement over the period. In an uptrend DI+ will be greater than DI-; in a downtrend DI- will be greater than DI+.

And now, the really neat bit...

The difference between DI+ and DI- will indicate the strength of the trend. The bigger the difference the stronger the trend. In a strong uptrend, not only will

DI+ be high, DI- will also often be low; in a strong downtrend, not only will DI- be high, DI+ will also often be low. And this difference between DI+ and DI- is called ADX, *Average Directional Movement*. It too lies on a scale of 0 – 100.

Assigning a cut off of 30 for ADX, we can define an uptrend to be in place if ADX is above 30 and DI+ is above DI-; we can define a downtrend to be in place if ADX is above 30 and DI- is above DI+. Note that the ADX reading above 30 does not tell us the direction of the trend only the strength. We look to the relative readings of DI+ and DI- to tell us whether it is an uptrend or a downtrend (which should also of course be confirmed by visual inspection).

Welles Wilder's book has worksheets for calculating all the relevant figures. However these days we are fortunate that most investment software will calculate and plot them for us.

Support and Resistance

I refer to support and resistance on a number of occasions, and provide a few further thoughts on the subject here.

One useful way to visualise the concept of support and resistance is to imagine battle lines between two warring parties–

- the **bulls** who are trying to push prices up, and

- the **bears**, who are trying to push prices down.

As the battle ebbs and flows, eventually a point will be reached where the bulls can push prices up no further, and the bears will succeed in pushing prices back down again. Another point will be reached later where the bears can push prices down no further, and the bulls will succeed in pushing prices back up again. These two points represent resistance and support.

Now imagine the battle returns to that same point, where the bears overcame the bulls before (the point of resistance), and once again the bears win the day, pushing prices down once more from that point. The resistance point has become stronger.

And then, later, the battle returns to the same point where the bulls overcame the bears before, the point of support, and once again the bulls win the day, pushing prices up once more from that point. The support point has become stronger.

Betting via Exchanges

Although betting exchanges haven't yet taken off for financial instruments, it might do one day, and experienced spread bettors will want to monitor the growth of this as a possible alternative to financial spread betting. At this point I offer a few introductory comments, in case.

How it works

Betting exchanges are a recent phenomenon, but rapidly expanding particularly in the sports betting arena. Since they represent a realistic substitute for spread betting for some customers, they are in this respect an additional competitive threat to the spread betting firms. This should add further momentum to the moves towards better spreads and enhanced services for spread betting customers.

With a traditional bookie, we as customers go head to head with the bookie. A net loss for the customers means a net win for the bookie, and vice versa. In a betting exchange customers bet against each other; the firm owning the exchange merely matches customers against each other. The bets themselves are zero sum (pre commission), for every £1 won by a customer there will be £1 lost by another customer, and the firm supplying the exchange neither wins nor loses. Where the firm makes its money is through commission – typically charging the winners 5%. If you lose a bet, or your bet can't be matched with another customer you are charged no commission.

Benefits and risks of this type of betting

It is worth looking at the advantages of this type of betting compared to traditional fixed odds betting with a bookie.

1. You get to choose the odds you want – the exchange will accept your bet request at that price providing they can find someone willing to take the other side – i.e. provided they can match your bet with another customer (or customers).

2. The odds on an exchange are usually significantly better than the odds you can get with a traditional bookie.

3. As well as "backing," (i.e. betting on an event happening), you can also "lay" (i.e. bet on an event not happening); in other words, you can take the bookies side of the transaction.

4. You can bet "in play", i.e. you can close bets for a profit or a loss in the middle of an event.

For an experienced spread bettor, the betting exchange offers a potentially new hunting ground with a number of advantages–

1. losses limited to size of stake, with no hidden extras (no commission on losing bets)

2. no spread betting firm spreads

3. odds generally competitive when compared to binary bets

4. no slippage and no re-quotes – what you see is what you get

5. other customers are involved in setting prices, as opposed to the professionals in the spread betting firms, so there are some bargains out there

6. you can utilise many of your usual spread betting entry techniques to establish when you want to bet on financial instruments in the exchanges

7. you can "trade" sports odds: simple example, take golf, the Open, you find one of the top players being quoted at 12.5 to back, pre tournament. You back. He makes the cut, and the quote is now 10.5. You can close out for a profit. You have traded the movement in the odds rather than backing the player all the way to the finish.

Possible disadvantages at the moment–

1. no leverage, so more funds required to trade equivalent size

2. upside limited to odds of original stake, however still possible to establish risk reward ratios to match personal preferences

3. commission paid on 5% of winnings – gross winnings not net winnings; this can amount to more than the spread betting firms' spreads

4. coverage much less than spread betting, good on the sports side, but minimal on financial instruments

5. potential liquidity issues except on the most popular bets

Overall, this is a fairly new market; but potentially of great interest to a winning sports spread bettor, and perhaps one day of interest to the winning financial spread bettor.

Directory Of Spread Betting Firms

The number of suppliers is growing and changing. As I wrote this book there were several new entrants. This list will therefore not be definitive, I offer it as a starting point for your research.

Spread betting

Alpesh Patel:	www.alpeshpatelspreads.com
Cantor Index:	www.cantorindex.co.uk
Capital Spreads:	www.capitalspreads.com
City Index:	www.cityindex.co.uk
CMC Markets:	www.cmcmarkets.co.uk
Easy2spreadbet:	www.easy2spreadbet.com
E*TRADE:	www.etradespreadbetting.com
Finspreads:	www.finspreads.com
FuturesBetting.com:	www.futuresbetting.com
Global Trader:	www.gt247.com
iDealing.com:	www.idealing.com
IG Index:	www.igindex.co.uk
Man Spread Trading:	www.manspreadtrading.com
Sporting Index:	www.sportingindex.com (sports)
Spreadex:	www.spreadex.com
Barclays Stockbrokers:	www.stockbrokers.barclays.co.uk/spreadtrading
TD Waterhouse:	www.tdwaterhousespreadbetting.co.uk
Tradindex.com:	www.tradindex.com
TwoWay Spreads:	www.twowayspreads.com
WorldSpreads:	www.worldspreads.com

Fixed odds

An (increasing) number of the providers above also offer binary bets or fixed odds bets. Here are some additional web sites of firms offering binary betting or fixed odds betting...

BetOnMarkets.co.uk: www.betonmarkets.co.uk

binarybet.com: www.binarybet.com

Blue Square: www.bluesq.com

Finally, here are some betting exchanges, if that is the way you have decided to go....

Betfair: www.betfair.com

intrade: www.intrade.com

Mansion: www.mansion.com (sports)

Index

Index

P

Q

R